Praise for *Think Like an Entrepren*

"Bev is the ideal career coach—full of i̶d̶ ̶ ̶ ̶ ̶ ̶ ̶ ̶ ̶ ̶ ̶ ̶ ̶ ̶ ̶ ̶ ̶ ̶ ̶ encourages and educates people—sometimes wit̶ ̶ ̶ ̶ ̶ ̶ ̶ ̶ ̶ ̶ ̶ ̶ ̶ ̶ ̶ sometimes
with a firm hand. But, either way, she gets people to where THEY want to go.
She motivates them to be the best they can be at whatever career they choose.
She also guides people seeking second and third careers in life. She works
under the philosophy that it is NEVER too late."

— Thomas Hodson, Joe Berman Professor of Communication, Scripps
College of Communication, Ohio University and General Manager of
WOUB Public Media

"This phenomenal woman has blessed me with her knowledge and expertise to become a better manager and a better person. With this book she can
do the same for you."

— Arlean Leland, Associate General Counsel, Civil Rights, Labor and
Employment Law, U.S. Department of Agriculture

"Reading a career tip chapter by Bev Jones is like having a wise counselor
with a gently authoritative voice sitting next to you offering the best advice
that money can buy and that you can realistically follow. A pure pleasure."

—Ira Chaleff, author of *The Courageous Follower*
and *Intelligent Disobedience*

"Bev is an amazing coach who reaches beyond promoting leadership and
excellent management skills to help her clients understand that it's not just
about success at work. She demonstrates that if you take care of yourself and
your health and your family, and you work on bringing other people up along
the way, it makes you a fuller, richer, better person. With this wonderful book,
Bev brings her insightful coaching to a wide community, including you."

—Sherry Little, former Acting Administrator of the Federal Transit
Administration, now Partner and Co-founder, Spartan Solutions LLC

"Career coach Beverly Jones will show you how to handle tricky challenges at work, make change your friend and, most of all, have the career you want and deserve."

— Richard Eisenberg, Work & Purpose Editor, Nextavenue.org

"Bev is an expert coach and a fine teacher who can turn academic research into sound, practical advice. She is amazing, and we are excited about her book."

—Dr. Mark Weinberg, Founding Dean, The Voinovich School of Leadership and Public Affairs at Ohio University

"Bev is a great coach, and every page of her book is teeming with insight drawn from her path breaking career in industry as well as her steadfast support of hundreds of clients as a leadership, executive, and career coach. Whether you're a client or a coach, read this book and prepare to drink from a bubbling stream of sound advice and inspiration."

— Coach Dave Goldberg, President of ThreeJoy.com and coauthor of *A Whole New Engineer*

"Beverly's book offers practical insights and tips grounded in decades of experience. Her pragmatic, thoughtful observations and commentary will prove invaluable to young legal practitioners, government and corporate lawyers starting to step into leadership decision-making. Her sage counsel and coaching will help make them better stewards of the future."

— Michael J. Zimmer, senior attorney and ABA Energy and Environment Section Committee past chairman of two committees

THINK LIKE AN
ENTREPRENEUR
ACT LIKE A CEO

50 Indispensable Tips to
Help You Get Ahead At Work

Beverly E. Jones

JAICO PUBLISHING HOUSE

Ahmedabad Bangalore Bhopal Bhubaneswar Chennai
Delhi Hyderabad Kolkata Lucknow Mumbai

Published by Jaico Publishing House
A-2 Jash Chambers, 7-A Sir Phirozshah Mehta Road
Fort, Mumbai - 400 001
jaicopub@jaicobooks.com
www.jaicobooks.com

Original English language edition published by
The Career Press, Inc.
12 Parish Drive, Wayne
NJ 07470, USA
All right reserved

To be sold only in India, Bangladesh, Bhutan,
Pakistan, Nepal, Sri Lanka and the Maldives.

THINK LIKE AN ENTREPRENEUR, ACT LIKE A CEO
ISBN 978-81-8495-847-8

First Jaico Impression: 2016

Printed by
Nutech Print Services-India
B-25/3, Okhla Industrial Area, Phase-II
New Delhi - 110 020

To my mother, Lorna Jones, who continues to reinvent her career
as an artist at age 95.

ACKNOWLEDGMENTS

I am so grateful to my husband, Andy Alexander, for his support. Of course, it is wonderful to have a resident expert editor. Knowing that he has read every word of the book and given me a thumbs-up is great for my confidence level. More than that, the two of us always approach careers as a team effort, and I appreciate his years of patience and support for this project.

I'm also indebted to my friend and frequent brainstorming partner Kerry Hannon, who wrote the Foreword and shared "Love Your Job" tips. Kerry convinced me that writing a book can be fun and manageable, and then she taught me how to do it. Kerry also introduced me to freelance editor Debra Englander, who helped me find my agent and then did a preliminary edit of the book. As a first-time author, I needed a lot of guidance, and Kerry and Debby helped me stay on track.

I love the feeling of being supported by talented professionals. And it has been such a pleasure to work with an assured, straightforward, competent pro like my agent Cynthia Zigman at Second City Publishing Services. Thanks for sticking with me and getting the deal done, Cindy. I already have thoughts about the next project.

I might not have kept going on the book were it not for the years of encouragement—sometimes even the kindest possible nagging—from a long list of family, friends, and colleagues. Special thanks to Ira Chaleff, Bob Deans, Emily Emmett, and Merry Foresta, who were kind enough to read early versions of the proposal and encouraged me to keep going. Thanks, too, to Sherry Little, Andrea Wilkinson, Gayle Williams-Byers, Bruce Jones, and Libby Vick for being my faithful cheering squad.

Ohio University is my home town and a center of my still continuing education. I so appreciate the support and enthusiasm of many friends there, including: Jan and Tom Hodson and many of Tom's colleagues and fellow alumni of the Scripps College of Communication; Mark Weinberg and his team at the Voinovich School of Leadership and Public Affairs; and JR Blackburn, Ann Brown, Sue Chiki, and the rest of the OHIOWomen crew.

Many of my clients have been part of this process. I won't mention their names, and the book's anecdotes have been substantially changed to hide personal details. But you know who you are. I'm very grateful for all the suggestions for e-zines, blog posts, and book chapters. Thanks for your interest through the years and for so much enthusiastic support for this and other writing projects.

Finally, thank you Career Press, for your confidence and professionalism.

CONTENTS

FOREWORD

When I hear people grousing about their jobs or their boss, I want to holler: Suck it up! Do something about it. Stop being a victim.

In my books, columns, and speeches that I deliver around the country, I dole out job advice for all workers from 22 to 82 and beyond. It's about finding meaning and joy in the work you do every day. It's about feeling like you're relevant and making a difference.

My career advice runs the gamut from helping people make the most of where they are right now, to finding strategic ways to pivot to a successful career change, or developing a strategy to reenter the workforce after a job loss, or perhaps to land a part-time job to earn income in retirement to shore up financial security.

Sometimes, all it takes is making small changes to how we work or view our work to get our mojo going.

Regardless of our career stage, we all run up against difficult bosses, feeling stuck with no signs of promotion, and feeling like we have no work-life balance, bored, and burned out.

For nearly a decade, one of *my* trusted experts, who I have consulted for several of my books and columns, is Clearways Consulting career coach Beverly Jones. She's my sounding board and my guiding light on many career and workplace issues, particularly as they relate to workers over 50.

I've found Jones' advice to be practical, straightforward, and frankly, doable. It ranges from big-picture soul searching to seemingly simple moves someone can make to get unstuck, such as uncluttering his or her office.

One keystone of Beverly Jones' motivational and knowledgeable counsel to her clients is to know that you "own your career." And in her superb and enlightening book, *Think Like an Entrepreneur, Act Like a CEO*, she has woven her concise advice together to offer hope and help to all of us.

When you change your attitude to Me Inc. and think like an entrepreneur, instead of feeling like a cog in the wheel, you're the driver. You run your career like a one-person business. You accept that no one else is going to do it for you. "Most of our workplace blues comes from a sense of powerlessness," Jones says.

Not only can this shifting of your internal thinking help you navigate your current workscape, if you're job-hunting, it can also ramp up your chances of getting hired.

Here's why: An entrepreneurial outlook gives you confidence, swagger, autonomy, and choice.

It works. Having grown up in a household where my father ran his own business, I was encouraged to think like an entrepreneur and to always have freelance projects outside of my main job. As a result, I've always been nimble and not entirely dependent—even psychologically—on one boss.

I learned to view my primary employer as my "client." It's liberating, and it has helped me navigate my career path and remain resilient during rocky patches.

By addressing the tangible challenges workers face, Jones' compelling book proves that by squarely tackling these internal and external shifts, it's possible to find happiness and success in not only our working lives, but in our personal lives, too.

"Do something every day to work toward your goal," she urges. "Once you have some picture of where you want to go, get things moving by taking small steps toward that vision."

Jones' mantra: What really matters is that you do a little something on a regular basis.

As the saying goes, a journey of a thousand miles begins with a single step.

Think Like an Entrepreneur, Act Like a CEO starts your personal passage to a better working life. Read this book for the inspiration, guidance, and tools to help you discover smart ways to take control and get your career in gear.

Kerry Hannon, author of *Great Jobs for Everyone 50+* and *Love Your Job: The New Rules for Career Happiness.*

INTRODUCTION

As an executive coach, I know the path to professional success isn't what it used to be. In many ways that's good. Today, there are more professional opportunities available than ever before. But in order to reap the rewards and enjoyment from a successful career, you must know how to acquire the skills you'll need for your journey, how to manage yourself in unexpected circumstances, and how to roll with the punches.

For decades I've worked closely with high-achieving professionals and I've learned that you can't predict where your career path will take you. But you *can* prepare for it. You can learn smart workplace tactics and, at the same time, gradually build qualities that will bring you success.

For much of the 20th century, success seemed to be a matter of climbing onto the right organizational ladder and hanging on. Professionals were expected to be loyal and conform to institutional values. In exchange for loyalty, big organizations offered the promise of lifetime employment.

Now, the idea of spending your whole career in one place, keeping your head down, and continuing to do pretty much the same type of work seems quaint. Careers flow through many phases, involving numerous relationships, shifting skill sets, and startling change.

Your career is likely to include many jobs. Perhaps some will be full time and long lasting, whereas others could be short-term, freelance gigs. There may be times when you juggle several jobs or businesses at once. Sometimes your career may not involve paid work, but your professional growth will continue as you go back to school, volunteer, or take on a fellowship as a way to explore new directions. You'll be in charge of your career. Nobody else will guide it.

And as you move from place to place, you may find that workplace cultures vary widely, making navigating on the job more confusing than ever. For example, you may find yourself in a situation where dress is casual, hours are flexible, and the hierarchy is loose. But although things look informal at first glance, you soon have to decipher complex relationships and meet productivity expectations that are extraordinarily high but never actually defined.

The whole concept of "career" is different than it was in the last century. When I talk about your "career," I'm not just thinking of what you do at the office. Your career is no longer distinct from the rest of your life. It includes everything you do to stay in shape—physically, emotionally, spiritually, socially—in order to do your best work. Your career encompasses your learning experiences, from the books you read to your circle of friends, vacation pursuits, and community activity.

"Professional" is another word that has shifted meaning. The traditional professions included doctors, lawyers, architects, and other specially educated, licensed, and relatively well-paid experts. But now the definition includes anybody who is seriously engaged in meaningful, challenging work. Today's professionals are committed to building their skills and expertise, and maintaining quality and ethical standards, in myriad fields from IT to the culinary arts.

And whereas modern professionals still want to be compensated, they expect more from their work—they want to find meaning and fun on the job, and at the same time enjoy a richer, broader life.

To get what they wanted from their professional life, your parents needed to demonstrate loyalty. But what you'll need for *your* varied career is to be adaptable and resilient.

Professionals who are "adaptable" are able to put aside assumptions about their tasks, bosses, or clients, and try new strategies to achieve what they want. They are willing to be flexible, sometimes experimenting a bit as they tweak their performance or build stronger relationships with colleagues.

Career resilience means being able to anticipate risks and feel comfortable with change. Resilience involves limiting damage during turbulent times. It means knowing how to absorb hard knocks, to regroup, and to bounce back when the worst happens. It's the ability to start feeling better and bolster your confidence after a setback. It's remaining engaged in the midst of shifting challenges. Resilience brings security in a constantly changing world.

My observation from watching hundreds of adaptable, resilient careerists is that, regardless of where they work, most tend to be entrepreneurial thinkers. They are curious, open-minded, and skilled at spotting trends and turning them into opportunities. They resist the urge to be defensive or get bogged down in the past. Instead, they handle each challenge as it comes along and then quickly refocus on the future. They keep learning and building their social networks. And they are open to new ideas, agile in tumultuous situations, and willing to keep building social, technical, and managerial skills.

In addition, over the long haul, the most successful professionals act like savvy chief executive officers. They are quick to take responsibility and are always planning ahead. They share the praise and turn quickly to problem solving when things go wrong. They know their own value system and they organize themselves to live within it. And they listen to other people and are typically eager to support their success.

Adaptable, resilient people may not start out that way

Resilient people aren't necessarily born with a unique ability to be flexible, bounce back, or forge ahead. Often, they are ordinary folks who gradually learn behaviors, attitudes, and work patterns that allow them to adapt as needed.

I'm a good example of someone who started out as a risk-averse worrier, but through the years became more flexible. At the age of 20 I was looking for a secure job track. But as it's turned out, I've reinvented my career again and again.

As an undergraduate at Ohio University, I studied journalism and planned to become a reporter. Then I was sidetracked by student activism to promote equality for women. That led to work in the university's administration and, at the same time, I became the first woman in Ohio University's MBA program. Eventually, I was called upon to take a fresh look at the university's employment practices and create its first affirmative action program.

From there I went to Georgetown University Law Center, thinking I'd settle down on a secure career track as an attorney. After a brief stint at the Securities and Exchange Commission, I went to a series of Washington law firms where I discovered that, in private practice, lawyers must be entrepreneurs. It was particularly tough for women to develop a client base and step into firm leadership, and during my years as a young lawyer I had some tough lessons about bouncing back and forging ahead.

Eventually, I was hired by my biggest client, Consolidated Natural Gas Company, to take charge of public affairs and policy. The leaders of that Fortune 500 Company had great integrity and were good managers. I enjoyed my work and found satisfaction in fighting for issues like the development of alternative power projects.

I thought I was at CNG for life, but then a corporate merger changed my plans. My job suddenly disappeared. But I was fine. As a corporate officer I was well compensated with a severance package and I discovered that I'd finally outgrown the need for a job that seemed secure. I decided to create a new career built around the activities I enjoy the most.

I realized that throughout my various jobs I was always fascinated by mentoring younger colleagues and helping guide them into leadership. So I went back to school, including to Georgetown University's wonderful Leadership Coaching program. And now for more than a dozen years I've been working as an executive coach, consultant, and speaker. I've worked with thousands of people, ranging from graduate students and young professionals to leaders at the highest levels of government, academia, and corporate life.

I've had an opportunity to help clients become more adept careerists without having to learn all their lessons the hard way. I can watch close up as they practice thinking like entrepreneurs and acting like effective CEOs. And I've seen how it is possible for people to become increasingly comfortable with change while mastering strategies for a flourishing work life and professional success.

What would it take for *you* to think like an entrepreneur and act like a CEO?

You may think you don't have the power, direction, or energy to create your dream career. And maybe you've never found change to be easy. But when, challenge by challenge, you learn how to deploy a broader range of workplace strategies, you'll get better at entrepreneurial thinking and acting like a leader. As you maneuver and succeed in surprising circumstances, your confidence will grow, and so will your resilience.

This book is a practical guide to help you become more nimble in the workplace. It will teach you how to build career resilience by overcoming common predicaments and by capturing opportunities, one by one. Though it draws on recent research and the advice of experts, the book isn't a theoretical treatise or an academic study. And although I talk about my experiences and those of friends and clients, the book is really about *you*.

Every chapter offers you simple, actionable tactics for tackling a career question that may be keeping you awake at night. The detailed strategies will show you how to:

→ **Handle specific workplace challenges.** One by one, the 50 chapters will show you how to navigate tricky career situations. You'll find practical answers for questions such as how to respond gracefully to praise from the boss, how to get over it when you don't get that promotion, and how to soften the letdown that comes after you finish a big project. As you master challenges like these, one puzzle at a time, you'll expand your set of career survival skills. You'll become more skillful at shifting gears and forging ahead. And with time, your resilience will grow.

→ **Create your own go-to change process.** A key to being more adaptable is having a comfortable way to get started when it's time to make a career shift, particularly if you find change to be difficult. The chapters will also help you to develop your own approach for analyzing work-related questions and finding ways to move forward. They will encourage you to think about how success might look in the future. And they'll show you how to create an action plan that can move you toward that vision of success. When you have mastered simple and reliable approaches to sorting out problems and making a change, you can face almost any career challenge.

Through the years I've shared these strategies with countless clients, so I know they work. Each chapter will help you coach yourself through an immediate quandary while creating the skills and awareness that will make you unstoppable. My hope is that—whether you read the book from cover to cover, or pick and choose chapters as you need them—you'll find lessons for a career that takes you where you want to go.

Throughout the book you'll find true stories about real people. Sometimes, particularly when I talk about a client, I have changed personal details to preserve confidentiality. In that case, the person will be given just a first name, with an asterisk to serve as a reminder that the name and personal facts have been changed.

I know from long experience that you *can* create the kind of career you want, and I've written this book to help you succeed in the kind of work that you enjoy and find satisfying.

1

To Launch Something New, You Need a Good Plan

Your long and varied career is likely to include a series of new jobs and other fresh starts. In 2014, the median time workers had been with their current employer was 4.6 years, according to the U.S. Bureau of Labor Statistics. And even if you defy the odds and stay with the same employer for much of your work life, your positions will change; you'll take on new projects, clients, or assignments; and your entire organization could be repeatedly transformed.

What I learned from my worst first day at work

My worst first day was 30 years ago, but it remains a vivid memory. I was a few years out of law school and shifting to a new firm in the nation's capital. The title on my business card read "partner" instead of "associate," in recognition of the clients I was able to bring along with me.

On my first day, I arrived in a new suit, with an empty briefcase, eager to make a good impression in the Washington office of this Virginia firm. But the attorneys who had interviewed me were all out of the office that day, and nobody else seemed pleased to meet me.

I found my way to the most senior Washington partner and introduced myself. He was curt: "At the interviews they all thought you were so great, but frankly I don't see it. You're going to have to prove yourself before anybody here gives you work."

The first friendly word was from the kind firm administrator who took me to lunch and warned me about a few things. She told me that there had been controversy over my title. And she hinted that in this male-dominated firm, both attorneys and support staff would need some time to get used to the idea of working with a woman lawyer.

The cool welcome was a challenge, but the most uncomfortable part of the day was that I had absolutely nothing to do. Well in advance, I had caught up with work for the clients I was bringing with me. This was back before there was a Web to surf, and I struggled to look busy. Instead of hustling over the weekend to finish my client work, I should have prepared a long list of things to do.

That night, I called my father, holding back tears. To cheer me up, he described his experience with new jobs: "The first day is always the worst day. The first week is always the worst week. The first month is the worst month. And the first year is the worst year."

I don't buy into the pessimism embedded in Dad's view of new jobs. But in that case he was prophetic. Within days the partners who had hired me returned to the office and greeted me with enthusiasm. And in successive weeks, months, and years I found my niche in the firm and eventually felt fully accepted.

My immediate anxieties were eased when I connected with colleagues who were more welcoming than the ones I encountered on that first day. But my time at the firm improved largely because I learned a critical lesson on Day One: nobody else was in charge of making me successful. That was my job. I went to work on my second day with the beginnings of a plan for how I would keep busy, take care of my clients, find new ones, and market my services to other lawyers in the firm. I never again assumed that the leadership would carry the responsibility for my success.

How to get off to a great start

These days it's hard to imagine that any established business would make so little effort on employee orientation. Often, in a process human resource experts call "onboarding," organizations develop elaborate plans to ensure that a new hire can quickly get to know key insiders and stakeholders, learn about performance expectations, and become familiar with the internal culture. Leaders may work hard to help recruits get a feel for the environment and develop realistic expectations about their roles.

But even when you're supported by onboarding pros and a welcoming boss, you're wise to have your own plan for starting your new job or assignment. *Whether you are joining a different company, changing slots in the same outfit, or launching a new project, consider these tips as you lay out your plan:*

→ **Learn what your boss wants.** Initially, your manager may be vague about what she wants you to do. Of course, you should ask about your expected deliverables and the best way to report on your progress. But don't count on clear, complete answers. Be prepared to do some detective work. Observe how your boss interacts with her other direct reports, what she typically wants to know, and how she sends information up the line. Notice her schedule, like when she seems to catch up on e-mail or which days she tends to work late. Get a sense of what *she* must do in order to be successful, and look for ways to help. Study the organization's mission and consider how your contribution— and hers—fit within the big picture.

→ **Get to know people.** When managers and professionals run into trouble with new positions or projects, it's typically not because they don't have the technical skills. Rather, they are more likely to fail because they misunderstand the culture or don't establish working relationships with the right people. During your first months, be methodical as you reach out to teammates and others who seem to have information to share. E-mail them, saying, "Since I'm new to this role, I'd like to set up a little time to hear your perspective and learn more about your projects and background."

→ **Listen and learn.** When you meet your new colleagues, ask questions and really listen to what everyone says. Resist the urge to talk about yourself and your successes in the old job. Keep an open mind, avoid offering criticism before you understand the history, and be cautious about choosing sides among warring factions.

→ **Set short-term goals.** As you start to feel that your feet are on the ground, create realistic objectives for your first few months, then for the first year. Reconfirm your understanding of your boss's expectations, focus on areas that seem to be high priority, and identify some relatively easy near-term achievements. Don't try to do everything at once, but identify specific preliminary steps—like introductory meetings—to move you in the right direction.

→ **Do what you say you will.** One of the worst ways to start out is to create a trail of broken promises. Deliver on every commitment you make, no matter how small. For example, if you offer to make a phone call or send along information, do so immediately.

→ **Be on time.** A simple way to demonstrate respect and enthusiasm is to meet all deadlines and show up on time for every meeting and appointment. This can be more challenging than usual if you're following a different schedule and you're operating in an unfamiliar environment, but it's worth the extra effort.

→ **Adjust your attitude.** It's not unusual to experience a letdown soon after you start your job. Once you're beyond the excitement of the move, you may realize that not everything is meeting your expectations. If you start to feel that the honeymoon is over, it will be time to make an important choice. You can give in to your disappointment and become preoccupied with how they've let you down. Or you can choose to focus on the positive aspects of your situation and commit yourself to doing what it takes to reach your goals. This is a good time to remember that you're the CEO of your career, and it's your job to navigate the bumps and barriers.

→ **Give yourself four to six weeks to work like crazy.** There's no way around the intense upfront investment required to kick off something new. This can be exhausting and isn't the best way to live for the long haul. But be super focused and consider working at an unsustainable pace for a month or so. For this brief time, you'll keep your weekends pretty clear, postpone social obligations, and skimp on household chores. At the same time, set a deadline, clearly marked on your calendar, for when you'll pause and reassess your work style. Consciously add back the things you temporarily cut from your life, and tweak your goals from this point on.

→ **Manage stress.** Adjusting to your new assignment will undoubtedly produce moments of uncertainty that can lead to a high level of stress. Select a strategy for managing anxiety and include a fitness program. You may feel like you have no time to work out, but that's shortsighted. The time you spend on keeping your cool and boosting your energy is an investment in your success.

Even if you're a person who enjoys change, starting something new can be unnerving. But once you are comfortable with your approach for planning and launching a new gig, your transition will feel less daunting.

Start your plan here

To create a quick and easy plan for launching a new job, answer these five questions:

1) What is my job description?

2) What are my most important objectives for the first year, including the things my boss wants most from me?

3) Who are the people who will be impacted by my work, who can help me to be successful, or who have information that I need, and when can I meet with them for 30 minutes?

4) What are quick and easy wins, including meeting people and learning about the job, that I can deliver during the first three months?

5) What organizational, fitness, or other habits will help me to perform at my best during the first three months?

2

Think Like an Entrepreneur, Wherever You Are

When I was in my 20s, it never crossed my mind that I would run my own business like I'm doing today. Back then, I wanted job security. And I felt secure at big organizations with clear and enduring missions like the Securities and Exchange Commission, where I worked right after law school.

It was flattering to be recruited from the SEC to my first law firm. But when I first arrived, I missed the roadmap to promotion that had been so clear in a government job. Then when I watched more closely, I began to understand the "rules." At the law firm, the partners with power were the ones with their own loyal clients. So, I began recruiting clients, not at first realizing that I was in effect creating my own little enterprise.

When I saw the chance to quickly become a partner, I took my clients to another firm, the one I wrote about in Chapter 1. On that first day, I still was thinking of the law firm just as I would any other employer. But I was immediately forced to see how my arrival appeared from the firm's perspective. The partners didn't view me as an employee so much as a very small business to integrate into their operations. As a partner I was obligated to market my services, produce billable work, and bring in more money than the firm had to spend in order to pay me and cover my overhead.

I gradually realized that every organization of any significant size is a collection of smaller operations, all of which have to produce products or services that somehow support a shared mission. Years later, when I joined my largest corporate client as the public affairs executive, I understood that I had to think like an entrepreneur in order to find success and real security.

At Consolidated Natural Gas Company, a Fortune 500 utility conglomerate, I was brought in as a change agent. I had to reorganize or invent costly outreach services, like lobbying on national issues and helping communities through our foundation. In every budget cycle I had to sell the CEO and the board on my expensive programs, always explaining how they would support both the company's service mission and its bottom line.

By the time CNG disappeared years later through a merger, I had developed a sense of what it's like to invent a business. And I was ready to try on my own.

How to think like an entrepreneur

Before law school, I earned an MBA. I came away from business school with the impression that some folks are born with an entrepreneurial gene, but the rest of us just aren't cut out for creating our own thing. However, today's view is that entrepreneurship *can* be taught. And entrepreneurial literacy will contribute to your success, regardless of your field.

In recent years, countless universities have created programs dedicated to the new interdisciplinary academic field of entrepreneurship. They draw students, from engineering to the arts, who understand that they'll always need the knowledge, skills, and flexibility to easily redefine their jobs or even create their own enterprises.

The fascination with entrepreneurship isn't limited to undergraduate students. Journalist and career guru Kerry Hannon, who penned the foreword to this book, has written extensively about how entrepreneurial activity could be the next act for millions of Baby Boomers. She reports that a rising tide of people ages 55 or older want to keep working on their own terms, and at times that requires starting a new business.

But even if you don't expect to ever create a business, developing a more entrepreneurial *attitude* could bring new vitality to your existing job. You might start your mental shift by imagining how it would be possible to reinvent your current job, change career gears, or launch a business or nonprofit at some point in the future. When my clients try to envision a different path, it often changes the way they look at their current environment. They may develop a more adventuresome spirit, experience fresh insights about their work, or connect with people in new ways.

"Intrapreneur" is the newish term that some use to describe the employee of a large organization who acts like an entrepreneur. That might mean inventing something new without being asked, or accepting the task of turning a rough idea into a profitable, finished product.

However we label them, I particularly enjoy working with clients who start thinking more like entrepreneurs. Even during the roughest economic times they keep bouncing back, whether by renegotiating their job to meet a new need or heading out on their own.

You can start immediately to develop a more entrepreneurial approach to your work. ***If you want to act like an intrapreneur, start here:***

→ **Know the mission.** Entrepreneurs tend to be passionate about their work. They set goals and they plan activities to support those goals. To be truly goal-minded, it's not enough that you understand your own objectives. You also should understand your organization's mission, the challenges it faces, and the way your contribution supports the collective strategy.

→ **Focus on the customer.** If you start a business, your customers will ultimately determine whether you succeed. Everything you do in a business must be focused on your customers. It's your job to know what they need, what they want, and what they think. And it's the same if you work in a large organization. Your success depends on the products and services you deliver to your bosses, your colleagues, and other "customers" as well. Ask yourself how you might better serve your current customers and look for ways to broaden your customer base.

→ **Understand business basics.** As a professional, you should be familiar with all the functions that make up a simple business. You need to be comfortable with commercial lingo and clear about how various businesslike activities are embodied in your organization, even if it's a government agency. Ask yourself: Do I have a mental picture of the operations that bring this outfit to life—everything from product development to budgeting, marketing, and sales? Do I understand the roles of support services like human resources and public affairs?

→ **Practice failure.** Successful entrepreneurs know that everyone has, and can learn from, false starts. When they experience a failure, they analyze what went wrong and apply the lesson to the next opportunity. There's a saying that "entrepreneurs fail their way to the top." But if you're used to success, you may become so afraid of failing that you won't take chances. This can stifle your inventiveness and limit your ability to collaborate and innovate. To mitigate your fear of failure, take up some activities where your success is *not* assured. For example, if you have no talent for dancing but your spouse loves it, sign up for a class. So what if you don't excel? The two of you will still have fun and you'll discover that it can be okay to not excel.

→ **Choose to be positive.** As we'll discuss in later chapters, the research is clear: you *can* learn to be more optimistic. Begin by noticing your own language, including the way you talk inside your head. If you are given to complaints, regrets, and self-deprecation, learn to let that negativity go.

→ **Build your brand.** Your "brand" is what you stand for, including your values, your personal characteristics, and the quality of your work. We'll describe in Chapters 4 and 5 how you already have a brand, but it may not be the one you want.

3

Listening Is Your Sure Fire, Go-to Career Strategy

In Chapter 1, we talked about how one of your most important strategies for launching a new job or assignment is to meet as many key people as possible and listen carefully when they're speaking. In fact, if I could magically give you one super career skill, it would be listening.

By "listening" I mean you not only shut your mouth long enough for the other person to talk, but you also shut down the voice in your head when it tries to tell you what to say next. You concentrate on the speakers, and you hear what they say even if it means you have to fight the urge to be defensive or interrupt.

Neuroscience and philosophers suggest that people go through life aching to have their concerns acknowledged and their presence felt. When you truly listen, you meet that need and connect with the speaker in a special way, even though it might not seem like it at the time.

Listening is so fundamental to human interaction that you can usually tell if a person is actually hearing you, or is just pretending. Research on "mindful listening" shows that speakers can sense whether the audience is paying attention or just waiting for their turn to talk. When you're really listening without passing judgment, you're more likely to be seen as genuine, charismatic, and even attractive.

Becoming a stronger listener is like building your physical strength. You build your listening "muscle" by noticing your reactions to a speaker and then putting them aside. For example, let's imagine your friend says, "You let me down." You instantly think, "That's not true!" But rather than butting in, you put that defensive thought aside and hear what else your friend has to say.

Then you could go further and encourage the friend by asking positively worded, open-ended questions. Instead of arguing, you might ask, "How might I have handled this in a more supportive way?"

You can sharpen your skill by practicing throughout the day in low-stress situations, such as conversations with a barista or sales clerk. For just a minute or two, give your normal concerns a rest and shift your focus to the needs and interests of someone else.

Great listening goes beyond hearing someone's words; it means noticing body language, facial expressions, and signs of emotion. It helps to be relaxed, so you might want to take a few deep breaths before starting a challenging conversation. A good way to begin a listening session is to summon up compassion for the speaker by imagining what it's like to see things from his or her perspective.

Times when exercising your best listening skill is a good strategy

If you want one essential ability to help you become more resilient, work on the habit of genuinely listening to other people. *Here are six situations where active listening is a particularly smart way to go:*

1) **When you're starting something new.** If you're joining a different team or meeting new people, it's tempting to talk a lot, to show off your expertise. Often, the better approach is to ask questions and demonstrate your strength by paying close attention to the answers.

2) **When you're a leader.** Listening is a core competency of leadership. You'll grow as a leader if you practice the discipline of letting others talk before you do. As your team members speak,

show that you're listening by nodding or restating a speaker's points. And find ways to let them know that you care about what they think, even though you may not always agree.

3) **When you're trying to make your case.** When we fall into debate mode during a meeting, we may ignore others' comments and obsess about the points we want to get across. Instead, it's more effective to understand our colleagues' goals and concerns so well that we can frame our suggestions with a minimum of conflict. Collaboration is a vital career skill, and it starts with appreciating the viewpoints of all the players.

4) **When you're in the middle.** Have you ever found yourself caught between two warring parties? You know it would be a mistake to take sides, but it can be a challenge to participate in meetings without seeming to align with one faction or another. The best approach here is to consistently present yourself as an open-minded listener. Let everybody know you're always willing to be fair and hear what folks want to communicate.

5) **When they're hard to get along with.** Once we start thinking of people as difficult, we may stop really hearing them. As they speak, we feel defensive and start working on our rebuttals. At some level they know we're ignoring them, so their obnoxious behavior gets worse. You can often defuse a tense situation by putting aside your resistance and concentrating on what is being said. By quieting your negative inner commentary, you may launch a new era of healthy communications.

6) **When you want to look confident.** When people feel insecure, they may chatter about nothing, brag too much, or insist their opinions are correct despite the weight of the evidence. Genuinely confident people aren't afraid to stay quiet. They already know what they think and now they want to know what you think. If you want to come across as self-assured, look for opportunities to shine the spotlight on others. Ask questions and be respectful of the answers.

Listening is a powerful strategy. It can help you understand what's happening, show that you care, and contribute to the growth of a supportive community.

4

Tweak Your Brand to Send Clear Messages

Do you feel squeamish when people start talking about "personal branding"? Maybe you think it means pretending to be something that you're not.

If that's your view of branding, get over it. There's the real you, the essential person that you are. And related, but not exactly the same, there's the professional. Your professional persona should be deeply rooted in your true values. But the person you are on the job is just a piece of your whole package.

Also, in your professional life—whether or not you know it—there's your personal brand. Your brand might be quite different from the essential you, and even the on-the-job you. Even if you don't want it or like it, you *do* have a brand. It's already out there, alive, and influencing the way people react to you.

Understand and shape your personal brand

Your brand distinguishes you from everybody else.

Originally, the word "brand" simply meant a name or symbol indicating the owner or producer of a product. For example, ranchers used hot irons to brand cattle so they could spot their own steers among the free-roaming herds. And back when soap was usually just called "soap," Pears Soap was named after the barber who invented a new kind of gentle cleaning bar.

Today, the term "brand" isn't the same as a brand name. In a "branding" effort, marketers try to distinguish a product, highlighting how it differs from its competitors. But the modern concept of "brand" is even broader than that, because it encompasses not just the qualities of products but also how customers *feel* about those products.

When we refer to a "brand," we're getting at something that reaches way beyond the actual product to include a full range of customer reactions. For example, the Coca-Cola brand reflects not just soft drink attributes and whether people like the taste, but also the emotional reactions customers might have to the happy messages in Coke commercials.

Your personal brand isn't the same as the real you, because it's defined partly by what people *think* about you. It's based on *their* assessments of your expertise, your work, and your character. Your brand is powerful enough to open—or close—career doors. But it might be quite different from either who you are or the high achiever you try to be when you're on the job.

In other words, even if you are a good person and you work hard, there's no guarantee that your brand reflects your best qualities and will bring you the career success you deserve.

This is a lesson that Sally* had to learn. She's a smart, tech-savvy, and collaborative project manager, but she'd been turned down for promotions. Beth, her manager, asked me to help Sally understand why she wasn't being taken seriously.

With Sally's permission, I spoke with some of her colleagues. Several described her as "a flake." Part of Sally's reputation was based on her appearance. She loves fantasy events and science fiction conventions, and sometimes she allowed weird fictional characters to influence her fashion style at work. Even worse, she bored colleagues by talking endlessly about the weekends she spent at shows related to her interests.

People liked Sally and found her amusing, but they thought her hobbies were silly. Sally's eccentric personal tastes had become such a big part of her brand that coworkers overlooked her strengths.

As we talked, Sally concluded that she didn't have to give up the things she loved to do in her free time. But she didn't want her passion for them to hold her back at work. ***So she launched a three-pronged plan to rebuild her brand within the company:***

1) **Manage appearances.** Sally aimed for a more mainstream personal style, so that her coworkers' reaction to her clothes and grooming wouldn't blind them to her competence. She began dressing more like her boss and she tucked her long hair into a neat French braid. She also stopped trying to interest work friends in her weekend activities.

2) **Build expertise and let it shine.** Understanding that it's not good enough to appear more like everybody else, Sally wrote a "brand statement" that described ways she wanted to be seen as unique. In particular, she hoped to be recognized for her technical abilities. She set the goals of becoming expert in a hot new technology and having her expertise recognized. She took an online course, kept studying and experimenting on her own, and published an article in an industry journal. As she learned more, Sally prepared a "how-to" guide for her colleagues and, with her characteristic enthusiasm, she said "yes" when they needed help.

3) **Show up like a leader.** Sally took a course that required her to start a leadership journal. As she wrote about the leaders she admired, she became more conscious of how she wanted to appear. She wrote a list of the leadership characteristics she most admired, looked at it frequently, and thought about it as she planned her participation in routine meetings. Visualizing the kind of leader she wanted to be helped her become more confident about her contributions and decisions.

Rather quickly, Sally changed her brand. Beth said other managers were talking about how Sally had "finally grown up." With her new, well-chosen expertise, Sally became known as an innovative thinker. Soon, she was assigned to a key project.

Try these strategies to manage your brand

To gain control of your brand, start with an honest assessment of how you come across. If you're creating impressions that don't serve you well, then it's your job to change them. ***If you're ready to do some rebranding, start here:***

→ **Research your current brand.** When marketers want to enhance a product brand, they may start with customer surveys. If you want a better sense of your brand, gather feedback from other people. On the job, this might take the form of a "360 review" in which your bosses, direct reports, and other colleagues are quizzed by a third party about your performance. A simpler approach is to ask colleagues how you might be even more helpful.

→ **Look in the mirror.** As Sally found, people are more likely to regard you as successful if you fit in with the crowd and look professional. Even in dress-casual offices, your aura of success is impacted by your personal style. People are influenced not only by how you put your look together, but also by the way you speak and carry yourself. If you feel that it's time for a make-over, find inspiration by looking around for people who appear energetic, polished, positive, and powerful.

→ **Promote your work.** It is not enough to build expertise and do good work. You need to share news about what you've been doing and learning. You could give speeches, write articles, or send out progress reports. Or you can show what you know in more subtle ways, such as offering your services to someone who needs your help.

→ **Shape your online presence.** The way you show up in an online search has become vital to your broader professional brand. When you meet someone for the first time, the person may have already Googled your name. You can't get around this by doing nothing. Your name is out there somewhere. An easy starting point for your online strategy is to create your profile on LinkedIn.com. If you can't bear to share, you don't have to complete the entire form. You can project your brand to the world simply by typing in a few sentences in the "Summary" section of LinkedIn's profile template.

Building your brand is the antithesis of being fake or manipulative. It's about becoming better attuned to how your work impacts other people, more aware of relationships, and more adept at understanding and displaying your inner self.

5

Start Now to Build Leadership into Your Brand

Lodged within your broader image is your brand as a leader. Your reputation as a potential leader may take years to fully develop, but it begins long before you manage a team or have a lofty title. Even when you're just starting out, your leadership reputation influences how much people trust you and whether they want to work with you.

It starts in small ways. You look like a leader any time you spot a problem, create a plan to solve it, and then execute your plan. You act like a leader when you treat other people with respect and you leave them feeling a bit more positive. And you can become known as a leader when you accept responsibility and follow through on what you promise.

As we discussed in Chapter 4, the full scope of your personal brand includes the impression other people have about you, from your clothes to your technical skills. The leadership component of your brand is particularly important because it's close to your core values. If you have a strong leadership brand, other people will have faith in your ability to deliver at a high level. Beyond that, when you're clear about the kind of leader you want to be, your own standards will help you to make decisions. And once you decide how you want to be known, it will be easier to focus on your highest priorities.

How to make leadership part of your brand

How people regard your potential to lead is a significant part of what makes you distinctive. Your particular aura as a leader may have a huge impact on the kinds of opportunities that come your way. *This four-part exercise can help you define and project a leadership brand that will serve you well:*

1) **Create your vision of leadership.** A simple way to create your vision of the leader you will become is to compile a list of personal qualities that you want to develop, and that you want others to see in you. Begin your vision by coming up with the names of leaders whom you admire; they could be teachers, bosses, or historic figures. When you've named three to five leaders, start your target list of personal qualities by asking yourself:

   ◆ What characteristics set these people apart?

   ◆ Which of these characteristics do I want people to use when they describe me?

   ◆ Which of these qualities sounds most like me when I'm at my best?

2) **Expand your vision list.** Review the following words and phrases that many people have used to describe effective leaders, and add to your own list any qualities that strike you as important:

   ◆ **Always growing.** The best leaders are constantly learning something new. It doesn't have to be job related. Your development as a leader is tied to your development as a person, and the growth areas you pursue in your free time can impact the way you show up on the job.

   ◆ **Self-aware and good at building relationships.** Research by leadership expert Daniel Goleman suggests that strong leaders are distinguished from the mediocre ones by their level of "emotional intelligence." And that means you have self-awareness, like noticing when you're too angry or distracted to handle a delicate matter. In his book *Social Intelligence*, Goleman says "we are wired to connect" with one another and by becoming more *self*-aware we get better at managing our interactions with others.

◆ **Positive.** A leader's attitude has an enormous impact on the team, and most people are more productive when they are around positive people.

◆ **Engaged.** To lead we must be actually focused on the people and activities around us. Other people can sense whether we tend to stay present in the moment, which can influence whether they see us as genuine and charismatic leaders.

◆ **Service oriented.** Leadership may begin with the feeling that you want to help others, perhaps by delivering what they need or helping them to succeed. The concept of "servant leadership" emphasizes attributes like kindness, trust, empathy, and the ethical use of power.

◆ **Well organized.** Good intentions aren't enough to deliver results. To achieve their goals, effective leaders develop work habits and systems associated with productivity.

◆ **Collaborative.** There's a big demand for people who can work well with others to achieve shared goals. One reason for this is that innovation is so often the outgrowth of a collaboration involving people with different views and skill sets.

◆ **Energetic.** To be at their best, leaders must manage not just their time but also their energy. This includes physical energy, which is linked to exercise, nutrition, and stress management.

3) **Study your vision list.** Now that you have a list of the leadership qualities you intend to develop, post it in a conspicuous place and look at it frequently, including each morning. Because we tend to remember pictures more easily than words, some people like to create an icon to represent the characteristics they're working on. Bill*, a client, came up with five attributes to define his

style of leadership. For each one he created a symbol—a simple picture—to capture a quality he wanted to develop. Because he's an avid biker and was training for a mountainous 100-mile ride, his symbol for "perseverance" was a triangle, representing a challenging mountain. Bill could glance at his sketch of those five icons and instantly recall the characteristics he hoped to develop as a leader. Eventually, to thank his wife for supporting his efforts, he had a jeweler find or create each of the icons in a charm. Then he was reminded of his growth path each time he looked at the lovely gold bracelet that his wife wore.

4) **Act this way.** A key to projecting your brand is identifying the attitudes and behaviors that will earn the reputation you want. Once your vision list is complete, a quick look will remind you of how to act. You might also consider a methodical way to practice the qualities on the list, one by one. If you're working on several characteristics, you might try a flavor-of-the month approach. Let's say you want colleagues to see you as reliable, creative, and positive. Go to your calendar and, for each of the next three months, choose one attribute to be your theme for the month. Now here is the most important part: If "be reliable" is your target for May, *commit to a specific type of behavior* to bolster your reputation for reliability. For example, you might plan to arrive right on time for every May meeting.

Your brand sets you apart from the competition. And your brand as a leader reflects and influences the way other people encounter your deepest values.

6

Power Up by
Tweaking Your
Personal Style

Did somebody tell you that if you work hard and do a great job, it won't matter what you wear to work? Sorry, that's just not the case.

The way you present yourself to other people has an impact on how they evaluate your accomplishments and potential. And your personal style—your clothes and grooming—makes a difference to the way you're perceived.

Obviously, your style is particularly important when you're job hunting or making presentations. Thinking about these occasions, I went to an expert, my sister, Libby Vick.

Libby spent 10 years in Washington politics and public relations, and for more than 20 years has been on the faculty at Northern Virginia Community College. In her business and professional communications classes, students of all ages and backgrounds explore how they come across on the job or in the job market.

Whether you're giving a speech or just trying to make a good impression, Libby says, "Your audience may focus less on your words than on your nonverbal message. In addition to things like posture and facial expressions, personal style is a part of that message."

Having a tasteful look doesn't require lots of money. Libby believes you can look smart whenever it's evident you thought carefully about how to put yourself together.

Women on a tight budget can still appear stylish. One approach that often works is to wear mostly black, or black and white. For men, dressing for success is both more flexible and more complicated than it used to be. A good tactic is to see how others dress and come up with a look that's a bit less casual than most guys in the group. But male or female, and whatever look you select, make sure your clothes are clean and pressed.

You'll feel better about yourself when you know you look good, and chances are you'll perform better as well. Libby says that in her early teaching days she didn't require students to dress up for presentations. Then she realized, "The speeches they give when they're wearing sweats to class are nothing like the speeches they give when they know they look good."

Libby says everything comes back to focusing on your audience and recognizing that all good communication is audience centered. So give some thought to messages you want to communicate and what your look will convey to the people you're trying to reach. If it's apparent that you made an effort, they may be more open to what you have to say.

Times to kick your style up a notch

Sometimes you feel too busy, tired, or disengaged to make an effort as you prepare for the workday. Losing interest in your appearance can be part of a downward spiral in your career. When that happens, a bit of a makeover might help you to break out of the funk.

Another time for a redo is when your career is on an upswing. A chic new look can be a subtle way to let the world know that you are on a roll. *And you may want to buff up your look when you:*

→ **Work with younger people.** If your wardrobe hasn't changed in years, they may assume that your mindset is back in the 90s, as well. Notice what your young colleagues are wearing and modify their choices to create a look that works for you. If you

don't know where to begin, ask for advice from a fashionable
friend, explore fashion blogs, or find a personal shopper.

→ **Work with older people.** It won't help your career if you look
like a kid. Get rid of the flip-flops if your colleagues will think
your informal dress suggests you don't mean business.

→ **Interact with clients or customers.** You won't make much of
an impression if you're dressed like you don't really care. You'll
be more credible if you look as if you considered all the details,
including what to wear.

→ **Are giving a speech.** Libby says it's tougher than ever to
make a presentation, what with audiences constantly yearning to check their phones. No matter how well you know your
material, you'll lose your audience at the beginning if you look
sloppy, uncertain, or unprepared. Dress up a bit in an ensemble
that makes you look good, and you'll get off to a strong start.

→ **Hope to move up.** If you're eyeing a promotion, dress like
you've already climbed the ladder. Instead of blending in with
your peers, take a cue from your bosses, or their bosses, and
dress as if you're one of them.

→ **Are seeking a new position.** In interviews, first impressions
are critical. And people will register how nicely you've cleaned
up, even before you open your mouth. Dressing conservatively
is often the safest bet, but you'll also want to look like you fit in
with the office culture. Being a little over-dressed is acceptable
because it shows the interviewer how much you care.

→ **Want to avoid stereotypes.** My hip mother, Lorna Jones,
passed her driving test at age 93. I asked if she'd been nervous
about driving with a motor vehicle department official in her
car, and she said it had been no problem because she was prepared. "I had my hair done and I dressed like a professional,"
she said. "After 80, if you dress casually or look untidy, people
may assume you have dementia." When you look classy, folks
are more likely to put their prejudices aside.

In a work setting, your personal image is part of your brand. It suggests
something about how much you value the work, and how you expect others
to treat you.

7

Talk Back to the Voice in Your Head

Throughout school there was a voice in my head saying, "If you don't study, you're gonna flunk." I've no idea where those words came from. My parents didn't pressure me about studying, but I heard the refrain every time I was tempted to skip my homework.

The voice seemed to fade away when I was an undergraduate, but it roared back when I entered Georgetown Law. I was excited to be in Washington and tempted by the leisure options, from museums to bars. That nagging warning, though, often kept me at my books. At times I even cranked up the volume, saying aloud to myself, "You're gonna flunk, you're gonna flunk."

After graduation, the message changed but the voice was more insistent than ever. During my early years in law, the message was often, "They aren't used to women here. You have to work harder than the men." The exhortations would wake me up in the middle of the night, and distract me in situations that should have been fun.

Eventually, however, I noticed that it wasn't the lawyers sitting longest at their desks who seemed to be getting clients. In a big "Aha!" moment, I saw that the tyrannical voice in my head could be wrong. Grinding out the written work mattered, but so did other activities, like building relationships. From then on, instead of always knuckling under, I practiced ignoring that voice, or even arguing back. When it told me to stay put, I might respond, "This dinner is a good opportunity and I'm going."

Then, as I summoned the courage to broaden my professional circle and pitch potential clients, I had to find ways to bounce back when people weren't responsive. I noticed that often, the worst part wasn't what *they* said—it was the scathing assessment from my inner voice. So I practiced ignoring messages like, "They'll never hire you," and told myself that disappointments are growth experiences. I would say to myself, "Okay, what did we learn here?"

Unlock new energy by managing your inner voice

Each of us has a repetitive voice in our head, commenting, warning, and judging. Sometimes the voice gets stuck in the past, perhaps returning us to moments that could have gone better. If the voice is preoccupied with things that could go wrong in the future, we call that "worrying."

Much Eastern philosophy explores ways to quiet the babble in your mind. Practices like meditation and prayer can help you stop listening to that tedious noise and become more in touch with a deeper, more connected you.

In the West, scientists have begun to understand the nature of our internal commentary, as well as the many ways it interacts with our physical health. It seems that the relentless voice in your head reflects not only your own past learning, but also the collective experience that you've soaked up from others. Some experts suggest that the voice evolved as a survival tool, and its incessant messages are rooted in ancient problems and dangers. At work, that voice can provide you with warnings and motivation.

When we're fully engaged in rewarding tasks, the voice may grow quiet. Too often, however, the whining monologue can become a nuisance, keeping us awake at night and subjecting us to needless worry. The voice can discourage us from taking risks, distract us from important work, and undercut our productivity.

The good news is that you don't have to let that negative self-talk exhaust you. *Here are a few ways to break free from compulsive negative thought patterns:*

→ **Just notice.** Simply observing *which* thoughts tend to recur can help break their hold. Identify the niggling phrases that flow through your mind most frequently. Each time one returns, just observe it and try not to react. Remind yourself: It's just that old thought and I don't have to listen.

→ **Reframe them.** Make a list of your recurring negative thoughts. Draft a more positive alternative to each thought on your list. For example, if you keep thinking, "This job is boring," your rewrite might be: "Today, I will take one step to make this job more interesting." When the same old thought occurs, counter with the revised version. Repeat the reframed statement over and over. With enough repetitions, you can replace the old message with the more helpful new one.

→ **Name them.** You can get distance from recurring negative thoughts by putting a label on each thought pattern. For example, you might say to yourself, "That's just my Monday morning chatter," and let the babble go. Another technique is to visualize the narrator in your mind who is voicing the message. Then you may be able to dismiss your worries by saying, "Oh, that's just my Monday morning Grinch talking." I love Rick Carson's classic book, *Taming Your Gremlin*, which suggests that you imagine how your internal narrator may look. By picturing your nasty little gremlin, you weaken its power to badger you.

So much of building resilience and feeling more comfortable with manageable risk is a matter of getting out of your own way. A good starting point is simply becoming aware of the voice in your head and recognizing that you don't always have to listen.

8

How Do Other People Get Self-Discipline?

Do you know people who have so much self-discipline that it makes everything look easy? Does it sometimes feel like your career would take off if you had as much discipline as one of your colleagues?

That was the case with Doug*, an energetic communications and marketing consultant. He is an expert in his field and his charismatic personality helps him to attract more clients than he can easily serve. He has a strong team to share the work, but when we first spoke, Doug complained that he couldn't seem to get organized. He had so much going on that he couldn't keep track of the details. Opportunities would slip away when he failed to follow up, and he worried that his disorganization would result in a serious mistake.

Doug would invent reasonable processes for keeping track of prospects and client projects, and his team would adopt them. But then he'd create chaos by ignoring his own systems. He'd fail to report on his activity, forget about his promises, or reinvent a critical strategy without sharing the plans.

"The problem is I just wasn't born with enough self-discipline," Doug said. "It's easy for people like my assistant Jane, who's methodical but not so creative, but I'm a different kind of person. So how do I get more control?"

It is true that some people, like Jane, are naturally methodical planners, whereas others, like Doug, are more spontaneous. But, by definition, self-discipline isn't easy for anyone. A common definition is that self-discipline is "the ability to motivate oneself in spite of a negative emotional state." In other words, self-discipline is about making yourself do things you don't feel like doing.

And there's no single strategy for boosting your level of self-discipline. One reason is that this elusive quality can take many forms. Sometimes it's about avoiding immediate gratification in order to obtain a greater benefit, like when you quit smoking. Another type involves doing something you don't enjoy in order to achieve a goal, like running every morning so you can lose weight.

But you *can* develop more self-discipline if you want to. As I explained to Doug, building your self-discipline is rather like building your body. Even if you're very weak, you can start today to build the strength of your muscles, one by one, and with time you'll increase your level of fitness. In the same way, you can start now to strengthen your self-control "muscles." By working on them a little bit every day, you'll gradually develop more discipline.

You *can* increase *your* self-discipline

As a young professional, Doug loved deadline pressure and was proud of his ability to respond to client emergencies. But the cowboy style that worked when he was a sole practitioner wasn't effective when he was trying to lead a dozen people. He began to see how one of the most important qualities for career success, and for joy in life, is self-discipline. He stopped scoffing at research that suggests people with self-control are happier, better able to handle stress, and more likely to reach their goals.

More important, Doug discovered that self-discipline is a *learned* behavior. It is something you can work on, issue by issue, day by day, freeing you from considerable anxiety and wasted time.

Self-discipline looks different for different people. For Doug, it began with a new practice of writing things down. At first, he started writing for 10 minutes each morning, planning out his day. When that habit seemed firm, he began carrying around a notebook for capturing everything from phone messages to commitments he made to clients.

Try this plan for building your self-discipline

The people who stand out in a competitive environment show up on time, meet deadlines and commitments, take on the tough issues, and do everything they promise. To be that kind of person requires self-management. *If you're ready to build your discipline muscle, begin with this 10-point plan:*

1) **Start with a goal.** Is there something that you would like to do, if only you had the discipline to do it? Let's say, for example, that you think your job would flow more smoothly if you could get to work on time. Decide upon a manageable goal and express it in specific terms, like "I will arrive at work by eight o'clock every day for two weeks."

2) **Visualize what self-discipline would look like.** Identify the steps that could help you achieve your goal if you did, in fact, have the necessary discipline. To reach the office on time, would you turn off the TV and go to bed earlier? Lay out your clothes the night before? Fill up your gas tank during the weekend?

3) **Choose discipline.** Once you have a detailed vision of how you would act if you did have the discipline, start choosing to act like that. The opportunities to practice will take the form of a series of small decisions, like whether or not to turn off the TV at bedtime even if something good is on. Each time you meet the challenge of choosing self-discipline, you'll be exercising your self-control muscles.

4) **Write it down.** Keeping some form of log or diary is tremendously reinforcing and can help you to gradually build your self-control. Once you've identified the decisions that will help you get to work on time, keep track of how often you make the right choice.

5) **Reject excuses.** When you're trying to practice discipline, there's a danger you'll be defeated by the voices in your head. Notice when you're tempted by internal arguments such as, "I'm too tired to get organized tonight." Simply by becoming aware of how you rationalize will help you to grapple with temptation and keep you moving toward your goal.

6) **Encourage yourself.** Make a list of the excuses that typically prevent you from acting like a disciplined person. Then, for each one on your list design a positive phrase to help you get past that

excuse. For example, if your inner voice says "I don't have the energy," tell yourself, "I'll have more energy tomorrow if I get to work on time."

7) **Remove temptation.** It's so much easier to be disciplined when your temptations are out of sight. If late night TV is what's keeping you from getting a good night's sleep, can you move the screen out of your bedroom? Or hide the remote in another room?

8) **Acknowledge the difficulty.** Supervising your own behavior can be exhausting. In other words, we can exercise self-discipline only so much and for only so long, and then we're too tired to do more. So when you're trying to change, recognize the challenge and build your muscle in small increments.

9) **Reduce the pain by creating habits.** When you're working on a new behavior, the first few days are the toughest. But repetition quickly makes it easier. You start going to bed on time without having to agonize about it. As your new nighttime ritual becomes a habit, choosing it won't be so tiring. Soon you will free up your reserve of self-control for another challenge. So after you start getting to work on time, you might turn your attention to something else, like working on your "to-do" list.

10) **Reward yourself.** Positive reinforcement works. Support your change process by finding little ways to reward yourself when you do well.

As you move through the plan, play with the process. See what works for you. Treat setbacks as learning opportunities. Building self-discipline can become a game, with moments of fun and victory parties along the way.

9

How and Why to Keep Smiling

There still are scientists who claim that humans are the only animals who can smile. I don't believe that.

Daisy, our yellow lab, has a killer smile. As she establishes eye contact, her mouth drops open and the corners turn up, wider and wider. When she gives my husband, Andy Alexander, her love gaze, his big grin mimics hers. The two of them may briefly freeze like that, with locked eyes and happy faces. At other times, Daisy's smile overtakes her body and—still looking Andy straight in the eye—she gyrates with pleasure, from her wagging tail and wriggling butt to her vibrating shoulders.

I've noticed that simply by describing a Daisy smile, I can trigger an intense answering smile on Andy's face. Because he frequently travels, on occasion I'll describe her smile as we chat on the phone. In my mind's eye, I see his face light up at just the thought of Daisy's happy look.

Although there's disagreement about the validity of canine smiles, it's widely known that the human smile is contagious. Dale Carnegie wrote about that back in 1936 in his immensely popular book *How to Win Friends*

& Influence People. In its section on "Six Ways to Make People Like You," Principle 2 was just one word: "Smile."

Carnegie said, your smile "is a messenger of your goodwill" and a simple way to make a good impression. He advised readers to smile even when they don't feel like it, because action and feeling go together. If you smile you'll feel happier, and those around you may as well.

Reasons why smiling is still a good strategy

In the roughly 80 years since Carnegie drafted Principle 2, psychologists and other scientists have undertaken countless studies of the human smile. It seems that the phenomenon is more complicated than Carnegie suggested. For one thing, your smile and the message it carries are shaped partly by your culture. For example, in the American South people smile more often, and to stone-faced Northeasterners, their friendly demeanors may come across as fake. Also, immediate circumstances can shift the way your expression is interpreted. Normally your smile is positive for the person who receives it. But if you walk around with a big grin after you get the plum assignment, it might get under your office rival's skin.

Despite the complexities, however, modern research affirms that "Smile!" is often excellent career advice. ***Here are some why's and how's of smiling:***

- **It's healthy and feels good.** Smiling can increase the release of endorphins and other mood-enhancing hormones. It can calm your heart rate and blood pressure, contribute to a heightened sense of well-being, and lead to improved health. Smiling can help you release tension and work-related stress with an impact so profound you may experience it at a cellular level.

- **You'll look good.** When you smile, there's a better chance other people will perceive you as competent, attractive, likable, and memorable. They are also more likely to find you approachable and see you as trustworthy. And they'll think you look younger. On top of all that, the odds are better that they'll remember you the next time you meet.

- **It's contagious.** We are hardwired to mirror each other's happy looks. When you smile at colleagues or clients, they may automatically return your expression. More importantly, as you exchange smiles with another person, the two of you connect in a more fundamental way. They actually experience the positivity underlying your smile and, as a result, could be more satisfied with your conversation.

It spreads. If your smile makes a team member feel good, his mood will improve and he'll be more likely to smile at the next face he sees. The wave of good feeling can become viral, moving from one person to another. The culture of your whole team can be improved by the addition of just one member who often smiles.

Even fakes work. The most powerful smiles are genuine, emanating from deep within you. But social smiles—those that require some effort on your part—are effective as well. And they can start a virtuous cycle. If you struggle to smile, but then I smile back, you will respond to my facial expression. Soon your tentative smile can become heartfelt.

You can get better at it. The more you practice a positive expression, the more likely it is that you'll experience spontaneous smiles. The trick is to start your smile from the inside, by thinking about something that makes you feel good. Simple techniques include summoning up the image of a loved one, or remembering a particularly happy event.

If you smile more regularly, your new habit can retrain your brain to see the world in optimistic ways. The more you smile, the more you'll escape the natural tendency of humans to focus on threats and other negativity. Your shift to thinking positively might boost your creativity and help you to be more productive.

An excellent way to support the habit of smiling more often is to consciously begin each morning with a smile. When you first wake up, summon up a happy thought and practice your best grin. Then your smiles may come more easily for the rest of the day.

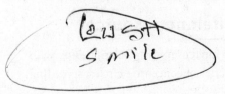

10

The Real Meaning of "Networking" May Surprise You

While working with clients, I've often wished for another word for "networking." Too often, the term seems to suggest a disingenuous glad-hander, talking too much and passing out business cards to uninterested bystanders.

That's the image that seemed to hit Jack* when we spoke about ways he could lay the groundwork for a job transition. When I mentioned the benefits of expanding his network, Jack grimaced and said, "I don't believe in that kind of thing. I've already got some real friends, and I'm not going to go to boring industry events just so I can try to make some fake ones."

Your "network" is a vital, lifelong resource

Your "network" is a complex pattern of interconnecting relationships with other people. You might visualize it as a series of concentric circles, spreading out from you like a spider's web:

→ **Circle #1:** In this innermost ring are your best friends and closest family. Many people, particularly introverts, prefer to spend much of their time here. But even dear friends move away or change directions. So one reason to stay engaged with other circles is to recruit additional folks to join you here with your home tribe.

→ **Circle #2:** Beyond your core group are newer friends, as well as people you've known for a long time but don't see so regularly. Here you might include coworkers, neighbors, and friends of close friends. If you don't make an effort to stay in touch, it is all too easy for members of this crowd to drift out of your orbit.

→ **Circle #3:** This large group could include dozens, hundreds, or even thousands of acquaintances from through the years. Among them are kids you went to school with, coworkers whose faces look familiar in the corridors, the members of your yoga class, and neighbors you wave to when you're out walking. They might also include people you've never actually seen, like your social media buddies, or colleagues with offices on the other side of the world. When you start thinking about Circle #3, you might find it to be a rich source of professional contacts with whom you're seldom in touch, but could be.

→ **Circle #4:** Your network expands considerably when you include people with whom you simply share a community. Maybe you've never met them, but you certainly could, because you hang out in the same places, belong to the same organizations, went to the same college, or work in the same field. You have something in common with each of these people, regardless of whether you've met or not.

Each of your Circles has a special role to play. For example, when you're seeking clients or a new job, you might wish to focus your efforts on #3. That's because the folks in #1 and #2 hear much the same news you do. Even if you're not on a job hunt, Circle #3 can be a source of support. Leadership can be lonely, and approaching your work with a spirit of self-determination can be isolating, but you'll feel less alone if you connect with your professional peers.

It's hard to overestimate the value of all these various relationships in your career and your life. In all four of your Circles you can find people who will give you advice when you need it, and join the party when there's something to celebrate. They are a source of career intelligence and many will reach out to help, even though they don't yet know you well.

So networking is not about superficial glad-handing. It means expanding your web of connection, thinking about other people, and caring for human relationships with the potential to support you in every phase of your life. And it isn't something you do in a panic, when it's time to shift jobs. You can build networking into your normal life.

Don't wait until a crisis to care for your network

When Jack* asked me to coach him in preparation for a job change, I knew he needed to discover how his social network could help. As things turned out, it did take Jack a while to build the momentum for his search. And then, unexpectedly, he decided to stay where he was, because his employer restructured his role.

Although he no longer was working toward a career shift, Jack elected to keep building his Circles anyway. He had come to understand how hard it is to overcome a neglected network. And, to his surprise, he'd found networking to be fun. Jack became active in an industry organization and joined a hiking club. Most importantly, he made the effort to develop deeper relationships with a number of colleagues and neighbors.

On the other end of the spectrum was Paul*, who spoke fondly of his network and seemed to treat it like a living creature. I knew that, without my prompting, Paul would open his job hunt by working his expansive Circles. He was well prepared because he'd spent years not only meeting more people, but also building on the many relationships he already had in place. *As Paul understood, there are two important ways to tend to your network:*

1) **Keep it growing.** Collecting more contacts is what people often mean when they speak of "networking." To count, this requires forging a small connection with another person. It's not enough to just hand your business card to strangers. You have to look them in the eye, find something in common, and perhaps make it into their address book.

2) **Build on what you have**. Networking isn't just about encountering new people. Also important is staying connected with the ones you already know. Because my savvy client Paul understood this, he could rely upon a valuable resource for his career quest.

A naturally kind guy, Paul's routine style was to mentor young colleagues, reach out to people feeling left out, and set up lunches with old friends who acted too busy to plan for staying in touch. Paul was always willing to help, and so, when he needed help, he had a long list of professional contacts who were happy to return the favor.

Building and caring for relationships isn't something you can do in a rush. It's a gradual process that you can actually enjoy as you fold it into your regular life. And if you keep up the cadence of your networking, you're unlikely to find yourself alone in a crisis.

Try these ways to nurture your network

In a political, career-focused city like Washington, watching the many styles of successful networkers can be fascinating. Some of the more conspicuous are born extroverts, thriving in a crowd and always eager for the next party. And some of the more successful are people who have been described as introverts— like Barack Obama, Hillary Clinton, and Laura Bush—whose well-planned social outreach helps them create resilient support systems.

If you want to become a more adept networker, test a variety of techniques and find ones that are comfortable and effective for you. *To get started, try these strategies for developing new contacts and deepening existing relationships:*

1) **Be helpful.** The essence of networking is exchanging help and support with other people. In a brief meeting, you might simply offer a smile or a kind word to another person. A key principle is to remain alert to small, easy opportunities to add value. Try these ways of being helpful to the people you know:

    ◆ **Make matches.** Become known as a "connector" by matching needs and resources and making helpful introductions. Perhaps you meet someone who is moving to a new city and you have a friend who has lived there forever and is always looking for volunteers for his nonprofit. By making an e-mail introduction, you can help two people at once.

    ◆ **Show up.** If somebody you know is giving a speech or planning an event they regard as important, work hard to be there. They may always remember that you made the effort.

◆ **Cheer.** If an acquaintance does something well, let them know you noticed and offer congratulations. Don't be afraid to show your affection and be willing to share in the excitement.

◆ **Notice rough patches.** If you see that somebody has hit hard times, don't wait for them to call you. Assume that they would be around if you were in need and reach out.

◆ **Volunteer.** There is no better way to get to know people than to work with them. So to break into a group, look for a chance to help with their project. This might mean offering to join a committee at work, or looking around for nonprofit groups that make a contribution in your community.

2) **Be in the moment.** You may have casual contact with many people throughout each week. But if you're like most folks, in some interactions you're not actually paying attention. Instead of listening, maybe you're thinking about what you want to say next. Or perhaps you're worrying about another project altogether. Get more from your routine conversations by working harder to focus. In each brief encounter with a casual acquaintance, shift all your attention on the other person. Instead of spending more *time* on networking, spend more *energy*.

3) **Network everywhere.** When you're in networking mode, it makes sense to vary your normal patterns and attend a wider variety of gatherings. But don't think of networking occasions as special events that you attend once in a while for that single purpose. Successful networkers get around a lot, and they engage with others wherever they go. Every time you are out and about, whether it's at a PTA conference or the gym, there's a chance to meet somebody who could become a friend.

4) **Know that every person counts.** The networker who comes across as slimy is the one who always tries to wriggle close to the most important person in the room. Classy networkers understand that every individual counts. And they all figure out that some of the junior staffers they treat with kindness this year may

be buying their product or running their company some time down the road.

5) **Turn enemies into friends.** It's okay to approach folks who once were your career rivals. As time goes by, petty differences are often forgotten and shared experience becomes more important. A person you once regarded as an adversary may warmly greet you.

6) **Work the crowd in smart ways.** Use these techniques for making a success of conferences and other events:

◆ **Put in face time.** It may not feel worthwhile to attend meetings or parties where you don't know anybody, but go anyway. In networking, over the long term, you get points for just being there. People get used to seeing you, and before you know it you're part of the regular crowd.

◆ **Plan before you go.** When you meet somebody at a professional event, they are likely to ask, "What do you do?" Before you take off to that conference, practice your "elevator speech" so that you can quickly present the best version of your story. And have some questions in mind, so you can deftly refocus the attention on them. Your questions needn't be job related. I used to play the game of seeing how many people I could get talking about their pets.

◆ **Take a few risks.** Know that most people feel shy at least some of the time. So if nobody is speaking to you at an event, it might be because they don't know what to say. Even if it makes you nervous, look for people who are standing or sitting alone and introduce yourself. Keep your list of questions in mind and accept the challenge of learning about them. Here's a moment to summon up a bit of your entrepreneurial spirit. If some stranger does reject you, just let it go; remind yourself that they don't know you, and it's probably about their problem, not yours.

◆ **Be willing to serve.** If you want to attract friendly notice, watch out for opportunities to do some of the work associated with the event. Conferences often give rise to follow-up tasks and membership options. So join committees, sign up for mailing lists, and volunteer for assignments, even if it just means carrying out the coffee cups.

♦ **Follow up.** When you do meet somebody interesting, find a way to stay in touch. Let them know you enjoyed the conversation, send along information they might use, and sign up for their mailing lists. And whenever it seems appropriate, write "thank you" and congratulation notes.

Are you ready to get out there and build your network? One way to begin is connecting with a broader range of your professional peers. Contemplate your Circles, and define goals for developing existing relationships or recruiting new ones.

11

What to Say When Your Work Is Praised

I grew up believing the proper way to respond to a compliment was with modesty. If somebody said, "Great outfit," my response was something like, "Oh, it was a bargain and I've had it for years."

As a young lawyer, if I worked long hours on a tough memo and a partner said, "You did a nice job," I was inclined to answer in the same self-deprecating way. I'd belittle my efforts by saying something like, "No big deal" or "It was a team effort."

My typical response was wrong in so many ways. For one thing, it lowered the partner's assessment of the quality of my work. Instead of reading my mind and understanding that I'd struggled hard to produce a first-class draft, he might take me at my word and regard the project as not a big deal.

Beyond that, when I deflected a compliment, I drained the energy from what should have been an enjoyable moment. The partner probably felt good as he approached me to offer praise. But then my response made him feel a bit let down, instead of more upbeat. I took the fun out of the exchange with my negative comment.

Not only was my response deflating to the partner, but it was also a missed opportunity for me. With my "no big deal" attitude, I denied myself some of the benefits a compliment can bring.

It wasn't until I became a manager that I understood how the compliment exchange should go. Both the recipient of the praise and the person saying the nice things should end up feeling better after the conversation.

To your brain, receiving a compliment is like getting a prize. Think of it as comparable to somebody giving you a little reward. And research suggests that you'll perform even better after *accepting* a reward. So your first step after hearing a compliment is to pause for an instant, focus on the good wishes that accompany the complimentary words, and allow yourself to accept the full value of the message.

Then, when you open your mouth to respond, you have two goals. First, reinforce the positive evaluation that led to the compliment. Second, make the giver-of-praise feel good, and thus more likely to offer you kudos the next time.

Tips on accepting compliments on your work

Once you understand what's at play, it can be quite easy to learn how to gracefully deal with praise from your bosses and colleagues. ***With a little practice, you can master these five steps:***

1) **Say "thanks."** Begin your response to a compliment by saying "thank you." And sound like you mean it. Even if a little voice in your head says, "I don't deserve it," or "He doesn't mean it," ignore your doubt. Smile and express appreciation for the nice words.

2) **Show your pleasure at a job well done.** It's not vain to acknowledge satisfaction with your own good work. After saying "thanks," you might extend the happy moment by adding a brief phrase like, "I'm proud of this one," or "I'm so pleased that I could help."

3) **Share the credit.** You don't want to deny your contribution. At the same time, you don't want to hog the limelight if that wouldn't be fair. If it truly was a team effort, spread the praise. Add a simple comment like, "I couldn't have done it without Tom—he was terrific."

4) **Return the compliment.** You can prolong the happy moment by offering a glowing remark in return. Say something like, "Your good advice made such a difference." But this works only if your words are sincere. Fake praise can be just another way of deflecting a compliment.

5) **Keep it short.** When the compliment exchange goes on too long it can become uncomfortable. If the flow of praise feels unending, it's okay to turn it off with a light remark like, "That's enough now. You're making me blush."

Manage your "impostor syndrome"

Sometimes high achievers find it extremely difficult to hear praise, believing they don't really deserve it. If you feel like an imposter, and not really good enough to deserve such a lavish assessment, know that you're not alone. A lot of amazingly successful professionals sometimes feel, deep inside, like imposters. Try to ignore your discomfort and accept the tribute gracefully. *You might also explore these techniques for becoming more comfortable when your work gets rave reviews:*

→ **Set specific goals.** If you define precise objectives, and your bosses agree to them, ultimately everybody will know whether you are successful. If you write down measurable goals, create an action plan for achieving them, and then follow the plan, your success will be hard to miss. You will find words of approval easier to accept when they clearly reflect the facts of what happened.

→ **Ask for details.** Sometimes positive sounding feedback doesn't actually feel good because it seems vague or overblown. If you feel like you could have done much better, but they say "terrific job," it is hard to know what's really going on. If you have a good relationship with your boss, ask for a more specific critique of various aspects of your accomplishments.

→ **Calm your self-talk.** Maybe the problem isn't so much their lavish applause as it is the retort from that pesky voice inside your head. If your habitual response to praise is to tell yourself "You could have done better," it's no wonder that you don't enjoy it. Notice your internal response to positive feedback, and practice letting go of negative refrains and replacing them with phrases like, "It feels good when they recognize my hard work."

When you approach your work life like an independent entrepreneur, and accept responsibility like a CEO must, there's a danger you may feel isolated. Part of the way you get past that is to learn how to easily accept and give feedback, not just within the chain of command but across a broader web of professional relationships.

12

Give Positive Feedback in Smart Ways

The term "positivity" includes a range of thought patterns and emotions including joy, serenity, amusement, hope, and inspiration. In the last decade or so, scientists have begun to better understand how vital positivity is to the quality of your life. First, of course, it feels good, and it can have a big impact on the state of your physical and mental health. Beyond that, it actually changes how your mind works.

From a leadership perspective, it's important to understand the link between positivity and productivity. There's no longer any doubt: Most people do their best work in an environment that's predominately positive.

It's crucial to be able to discuss your team's projects in an honest way, of course, and sometimes the news is bad. But the constructive approach is to focus criticism on the work product itself, rather than on the person. And when possible, the negative assessments should be framed within a generally positive dialogue.

The human brain tends to over focus on negative cues. This may be a result of evolution. Our ancestors, who were alert to threats like lurking animals, may have survived at a higher rate than their less aware peers, who died out. In today's workplace, this tendency means that your colleagues probably over focus on negative feedback. On a day where half the boss's comments are critical, they may go home feeling like they heard not a single kind word.

Some research suggests that workers are most effective in an environment where about 80 percent of the feedback is positive. This is something not understood by Josh*, a client who was general counsel of a federal agency. He came to coaching after a staff survey suggested that many lawyers working for him felt under appreciated. They were disengaged, their morale was low, and they had real concerns about his leadership style.

Josh's initial reaction was defensive and disdainful. He said, "Grown-up lawyers shouldn't expect to be thanked just for doing excellent work. They get paid, don't they? And when I don't comment, they should know everything is okay, because I always tell them when they screw up."

We spoke about the human need to be acknowledged and appreciated. And I pointed to numerous studies demonstrating that people will be more productive in a positive work environment.

Eventually, Josh agreed to try an experiment. Every workday he put three coins in his pocket. Each time he thanked or complimented a team member he could remove one coin. And he couldn't go home until all three were gone. After the first week, Josh said he was enjoying the experiment more than he had expected. But he still felt awkward saying "good job" and "thanks," so he looked for more occasions to practice. He found times to offer compliments and say "thank you" at home, in the local cafe, and wherever he went on the weekend.

The more Josh practiced, the more comfortable he felt giving positive feedback. And he was having fun with it. "The amazing thing is not that it makes them happy, but that it makes me happy, too," he said. Soon, he quit carrying the coins because he no longer needed them. Josh said he was addicted to his "thank you" habit, and it had changed the way he looked at several parts of his life.

Well-crafted words of thanks and praise can serve as powerful positive reinforcement, guiding members of your team to achieve, change, and grow. By regularly thanking or acknowledging people for their work, you can help to shape a more positive and collaborative office culture, even if you're not the boss.

Build your "thank you" habit into a powerful leadership tool

There's some art to giving feedback that motivates and empowers the recipient. It has to be real and focused. *Practice these eight tips for giving feedback in a way that encourages people to do even better:*

1) **Be sincere.** Disingenuous flattery doesn't work. It sounds creepy and seldom fools people—at least not for long. Get in touch with your sense of gratitude when you express thanks, and speak honestly about how you feel.

2) **Be specific.** A vague, casual "thanks" isn't nearly as effective as a more detailed comment. After saying "good work," add more particulars such as, "I particularly appreciated the way you involved other team members." Precise comments not only carry more impact, but also provide powerful reinforcement for the performance you want to encourage.

3) **Fully engage.** Part of the power of saying "thank you" comes from the fact that you care enough to focus on another person. Get full value from the thanks exchange by making eye contact and listening carefully to any response.

4) **Notice what's taken for granted.** If we always perform at a stellar level, our colleagues may assume that our high standard is just normal and cease to notice it. Then it feels especially good if someone recognizes how hard we've worked to keep up the pace. When you express appreciation to a valuable team member, make it clear that you understand what goes into their good results.

5) **Calibrate your "thank you."** Elaborate kudos in response to some little thing may seem fake and can be embarrassing. And too little gratitude for a huge effort can feel insulting. The tone and style of your tribute should be commensurate with the good work you're calling out. A casual e-mail can be enough to make somebody feel appreciated for a routine task. But a face-to-face encounter is more appropriate if they pulled out all the stops.

6) **Write.** Don't forget the power of a handwritten note. It still feels good when another person takes the time to sit down and write about what we've done.

7) **Be surprising.** Formalized praise, such as during an annual review, is important, but it's not enough. With time, routine assessments feel ho-hum, no matter how positive they may be. To show you mean it, express your gratitude or admiration when it's not expected.

8) **Be quick.** Offer your commendation as soon as possible after the activity that inspired it. Words of thanks and approval (like other feedback) have more impact right after we've done the work.

The "thank you" habit can be good for you

When you regularly look for opportunities to express appreciation, you are more likely to focus on and support the values and activities that matter most.

And research suggests that taking the time to feel grateful can actually reduce your anxiety. Saying kind words to others can feel very good, and sometimes hearing their response can feel even better.

13

Get Over Your Fear of Looking Like a Suck-Up

One of the greatest TV characters ever was Eddie Haskell, Wally Cleaver's oily, conniving friend, still to be seen on reruns of *Leave It to Beaver*. Eddie was an archetype who no decent person wants to resemble—a two-faced sycophant, always scheming and currying favor to promote his plans.

The fear of looking like a brown-noser is so powerful among professionals that sometimes they shy away from obvious opportunities to make a friend or pursue a goal. Among my clients, the people who seem most likely to worry about resembling Eddie Haskell are the straight shooters who look the least like him.

A good example is Trish*, a quiet but talented financial wizard who wanted to eventually move to her dream job in another division of the company. Trish said she'd probably need support from Al, a senior colleague who knew the leaders there. She described Al as smart and accomplished, but self-absorbed and eager to be the center of attention.

I suggested Trish find ways to build her relationship with Al, and speculated that he might respond well to a bit of flattery. She said, "Yep—he probably would. But I couldn't do it. I just don't like to suck up."

Even though it could mean a lot for her future, Trish didn't want to cultivate a friendship with Al because he seemed arrogant and might expect her to kowtow. I said she needn't grovel and asked her to simply make a list of Al's strengths and areas of expertise. Next, I suggested she spot opportunities where Al's advice might actually be helpful.

Trish identified Al's types of special knowledge and found projects where she could use his insights. Then she began to ask him for occasional guidance. To her surprise, Al responded warmly and eventually became her mentor. Ultimately, he guided her into the transfer she'd been seeking. Trish's reluctance to appear unctuous had almost prevented her from getting to know the man who became her champion.

Trish is not alone. Modest but otherwise self-aware people often have a disproportionate fear of looking like a bootlicker.

Are you reluctant to offer a heartfelt tribute for fear it will be taken as apple-polishing?

Do you avoid voicing sincere admiration because people might think you have a hidden agenda? If so, you're probably overreacting. There are many times when offering a compliment is an authentic move, and it's wise to get beyond your fear of kissing ass. *Here are seven situations when you should stop worrying about seeming to suck up:*

1) **When you're supporting a positive environment.** As I mentioned in Chapter 12, research suggests people are more productive in a workplace where most of the comments are affirmative. If you consistently contribute to the environment by keeping most of your words authentically upbeat, people won't regard your praise as manipulative.

2) **When it's a boss.** Are you reluctant to say "good job" to the big boss because you don't want to seem sycophantic? Well, consider what it's like from that boss's perspective. Maybe she worked her way into this job because she's the kind of person who is motivated by getting As. Now, however, if everybody is afraid to applaud her achievements, she may start to feel unappreciated. It's not healthy

or smart when the whole team is reluctant to give a leader honest positive feedback. Stop being so self-conscious and allow yourself to be as nice to your boss as you are to your other colleagues.

3) **When you want to make new friends.** As long as you're not being untruthful or over-the-top, it's okay to express respect or gratitude to a person you'd like to know better. Finding something nice to say is a polite and acceptable way of building a relationship.

4) **When it's wise to avoid conflict.** Some people are never going to be your friends, but you have to find a way to get along with them anyway. If they are annoying, you may make things even worse if you indulge in complaints. If they are bullies, you may attract more torture if you let them see your pain. When you're dealing with difficult people, a good starting point can be to talk yourself into a mood of relaxed confidence. Then look for the good things about them, so you can diffuse the tension with a compliment that is genuine and on target.

5) **When you owe them an apology.** There are moments when groveling is justified, such as when you forgot an important deadline, or said something dreadful at the office holiday party. It's okay to cringe and humble yourself when you want forgiveness for doing something truly wrong.

6) **When it would be kind.** It is always appropriate to put people at ease or calm their anxiety, regardless of their rank or yours. If empathy makes you want to offer a flattering remark, don't be put off by concern about how observers may judge your motives. And if you can't say anything nice, maybe you really shouldn't say anything at all.

7) **When you feel shy.** When some people say, "I don't want to suck up," the real truth is that they are afraid to step forward. When you hesitate to speak up, look more closely at your motives. Do you actually think it would look bad or is it just that the thought of drawing attention to yourself gives you butterflies? It's okay to be fearful, but make a smart, conscious choice about how you will respond to that fear.

If you honestly mean it, don't hold back from offering praise or thanks just because cynics might criticize you.

14

Use Games to Create Power and Direction

George*, a fairly new manager, hesitated when I asked him about his work. Then he said, "Objectively, it's going really well. But I don't know how long I can stand it."

The good news was that, after two years of building collaboration and creating expertise, George's team was exceeding all its objectives and had been recognized as a shining "center of excellence" within the large organization.

However, now leaders in other divisions were trying to steal some of the glory and resources. They were attempting to poach George's expert staff members by having them reassigned away to other challenges. When I asked George how many team members he'd actually lost, he said, "None. But I'm so exhausted from the constant fight to protect them that I'm not sure if I can keep this up. The stress is just too much."

I thought about how much George loves board games and recalled a party where he and friends had played fiercely for hours. The intense players shouted and mocked each other. But at the end of the game they laughed about the competition and talked about what fun it had been.

I asked George whether he could take a step back from the challenges to his team and view his colleagues more like other players in a strategic game, such as the kind he enjoyed playing with his buddies. George realized that he was finding the battles at work to be tiring because they had begun to seem too personal. It felt like a slap to the face when other managers responded to his success by threatening the important program he had built so carefully.

George resolved to start taking office politics more lightly, like playing a game. He would remind himself that decisions impacting his program reflected complex patterns and were seldom about him. He became more adept at quickly disengaging from daily skirmishes and regularly stepping back and refocusing on his bigger goals. As he concentrated on keeping perspective, George found work to be fun again, and less stressful.

How to invent career games to generate energy

A game involves goals, challenges, rules, and often interaction with other players. If you're struggling to understand a problem at the office, or if you're just bored by the daily drill, try approaching parts of your work as a game. *These tips will help you to launch your game:*

→ **First, define the rules.** If a workplace issue feels like a confusing mess, look at it in a different way by framing it as a game you must learn to play. Ask yourself: What are my goals? What moves will take me in that direction? Who are the other players? What are the consequences of each type of move? Are some moves out of bounds?

→ **Play more than one game at a time.** There was a time when George was torn. His ultimate career goal was to get a prestigious government job. But it felt like he was cheating his employer when he shifted his focus from current responsibilities to building his profile in broader circles. He said, "My career took off when I finally realized that it's okay to play two games at the same time. Every morning I not only thought about how to excel at my day job, but also visualized how to prepare for my dream job. That additional target and drive made me a better employee at the same time it opened doors for the future."

→ **Understand others' games.** In your workplace you are seldom in direct competition with your colleagues. It's like you
are playing your games, and they are playing theirs, and you
occasionally bump into each other on the field. The best players
try to understand their colleagues' goals and look for ways to
offer help. Collaboration happens when you see how your goals
overlap and find ways to play together.

→ **Make work more fun.** If work feels boring, think up a game
that will make it more interesting. Challenge yourself to do
something faster, better, or in a different way. Set a goal that
involves learning a new skill, varying your habits, or broadening
your network. As you find ways to make your tasks more interesting and enjoyable, you'll become more productive.

→ **Track results.** "Gamify" is a term used to describe the application of game design to a non-game process. Often, the idea
is to give you a real-time view of your own or someone else's
performance. People have embraced the concept of gamification
in the context of exercise, where wearable devices track every
step and can share summaries among selected friends. Some
employers are gamifying repetitive and boring tasks by sharing performance metrics among workers, hoping a little healthy
competition will make work more engaging. You can gamify
your own tedious tasks by keeping track of your performance
and rewarding your achievements.

If you think about your career as a very long-term game, you'll be less
likely to become bogged down in this week's problems. Regularly ask yourself
where you'd like to be a few years down the road, and create a game to help
you develop the skills and resources that will get you there.

15

Be Prepared with Clever Ways to Brag

What if a headhunter calls today with an interesting job possibility? Can you speedily show that you're an ideal candidate? And will you be ready if a boss or client has questions about how you've been using your time?

New opportunities or unexpected challenges can pop up fast. But when you're asked to quickly explain what you've been doing on the job, you might not be prepared to gracefully describe your achievements. Some people even go blank when asked to talk about what they've done lately.

To keep moving ahead in your career, you must know how to describe where you've been. Even if you're happily entrenched in a job that feels secure, on occasion you'll need to demonstrate your worth. Perhaps you'll want to go after a raise or promotion, or show that you're ready to take on a juicy assignment.

Even if other people aren't inquiring about how you're doing, to keep growing on the job it's wise to maintain a realistic sense of your current productivity. And if you routinely keep track of which activities bring the most results, you'll know how to prioritize your time in the future.

So that you're always prepared to demonstrate your accomplishments, consider these strategies:

→ **Keep a "love me" file.** This is a handy place—also known as a "brag file"—where you immediately store a copy of any document that says something nice about you. I've seen a few "love me" files that are full of handwritten "thank you" notes and letters of praise from grateful clients. It's more likely that your file—whether it's in your desk drawer or the Cloud—will be a mixed bag. Include anything that commemorates good work or a positive evaluation, from casual "thanks" messages to press clips or training course certificates. If your file is empty, you might think about rounding up letters of reference or testimonials, just in case.

→ **Get real about "performance management."** Your organization may have an annual performance appraisal process. Typically, it begins with the establishment of goals and ends when your progress toward those goals is evaluated in the context of a discussion about compensation. Often, the process is pro forma and nobody pays much attention to it. But that's a missed opportunity. Take charge of the process and use it to get buy-in for things you want to do. Propose meaningful goals and routinely document your progress. Your records will help you create a specific picture of your most important contributions.

→ **Count activities and results.** Your resume, activity reports, and project summaries will be more useful and impressive if you include relevant numbers. Let's say you're a PR manager and a prolific writer. You can tell a prospective employer that you blog frequently and write lots of press releases. But wouldn't it be more effective to say that in the last six months you've posted 60 blog items, averaging 20,000 views each, and you've sent out 83 releases resulting in at least 327 media clips? If you keep a running log of frequent and important activities, you'll always be able to show off what you've done in a powerful, streamlined way.

→ **Note problems and solutions.** Not everything you deal with generates good fodder for your "love me" file. At times you may have to address controversies, complaints, or even clean up a mess after you make the wrong call. Smart professionals face up to tough issues and find a way to remedy errors. As time goes by, however, other people may remember the problem, but not what was done to manage it. So you may need a record of matters you've successfully handled.

If you record your activity as you go along and keep track of the positive feedback, you'll always be able to produce a quick summary of your career highlights. Beyond that, your files will bring insights into how you do your best work and reassure you when you feel discouraged.

16

Get the "It" Factor: Create Presence

C lients whom I'm coaching often ask, "How do I get executive presence?" The question is tricky because "executive presence" isn't easily defined. Most folks agree that leaders need it and great leaders have it. But it's not so simple to deconstruct its elements.

Your definition may be based on a leader you know who has a commanding aura. You know what I mean—someone who exudes confidence and attracts people like a magnet. Sometimes the value of executive presence seems most obvious when it's missing. I'm thinking of Ed*, a brilliant corporate attorney who was repeatedly overlooked when spots opened within his company's management ranks. When I asked the COO whether Ed was likely to be promoted, she said, "No. He'll always be valued as a talented technical lawyer, but we're not going to move him up. Ed just doesn't have executive presence."

The COO didn't try to define "executive presence," but I knew what she meant. The attorney could write memos like a dream. When asked a question, however, he seemed hesitant. He'd mumble, then he'd shuffle down the hall.

He just didn't have "It." He didn't radiate that assurance, that dignity, that sense of control that others see as "executive presence."

Use this checklist to build presence

Do you sometimes worry that you don't have enough of that "It" factor? Do you fear you'll miss out on career opportunities, despite your great work, because you lack a powerful demeanor? Presence is an elusive quality, like love or happiness; you can't just pick some up. But you *can* do a great deal to appear more like a leader. You can build your presence by changing the ways you look and behave, and even how you think and feel about yourself.

Here's a checklist of key factors that contribute to executive presence. If you want to enhance your gravitas, read through the questions and find points to work on:

1) **Do you have a leadership vision?** As we discussed in Chapter 5, it's easier to act like a leader when you have a clear sense of the attributes of leadership. If you can't easily describe your vision of a leader, list characteristics you admire, such as reliability, honesty, or a positive attitude. Look at your list frequently so that you're reminded to incorporate these traits into your daily behavior.

2) **Do you seem organized?** If you're typically late, if your papers are a mess, and if you have trouble meeting deadlines, then your presence is compromised. Colleagues may see you as disorganized and unable to get the job done. Suzy* is a communications consultant who thought of herself as a ditzy, creative type. She'd explain away her lateness by saying, "Oh, you know us artists." But finally she realized that her firm's partners regarded her as a bit out of control. She saw they weren't going to promote her to the role of client manager until something changed. Suzy got her calendar and other systems in order. And, significantly, she told all her colleagues that she was working with a coach to become more productive and organized. She reshaped her brand, and soon she was managing client accounts.

3) **Do you need a makeover?** It may not be fair, but physical appearance is an integral part of presence. To look like an executive, it helps to be well groomed and well dressed. If your clothes

are dated and untidy, or your hair is always messy, you may come across as unpolished and not management material.

4) **Can you make a presentation?** The ability to give a speech or contribute useful remarks at a meeting will enhance your presence. Of course, you have to be clear and concise. But it's also important to know how to engage with other people. Present your points in a way that makes them relevant to the audience. Listen carefully to questions and comments, and respond without becoming defensive.

5) **Do you say what you mean?** Whether you're speaking to a crowd or chatting one-on-one, you'll have more gravitas if you speak directly, without hesitation or self-deprecation. Ask colleagues to observe the way you talk, so they can help you spot self-critical phrasing or annoying habits like starting sentences with phrases like, "I'm not an expert, but . . ." If you sound like you're uncertain of what you're saying, you can't expect others to be convinced.

6) **How's your vitality?** Managing your presence requires taking charge of your energy level. If you're sleep deprived, bored, or out of shape, you're less likely to come across as a leader. Being frantic isn't good either, because your hyperactivity can translate into stress for those around you. To appear more powerful, be serious about maintaining good health and fitness, and stay calm with practices like meditation.

7) **Do you know how to appear more confident?** People with executive presence seem cool and ready to handle any situation. But a superb record may not be enough to give professionals a belief in their own ability to master the next crisis. And even if they do know they can perform, that knowledge may not be apparent to others. A good starting point for boosting your confidence level, and making sure it shows, is to manage the voice in your head, as we discussed in Chapter 7.

8) **What's your body saying?** Your nonverbal behavior can be even more important than your words. At least on an unconscious level, people make judgments based on your posture, facial expressions, and even your fleeting microexpressions. They may even "mirror" your smile or the way you are holding your

body, with their emotions shifting to more closely match yours. And, according to fascinating research from psychologists like Harvard's Amy Cuddy, your *own* brain also picks up those messages from your body and face. If you assume the stance of a confident person, your mind and emotions may follow, helping you to soon feel more confidence.

Although the concept of presence is complicated, I've seen professionals make speedy improvements in the way they come across. For example, there's Lydia*, an accomplished economist whose concern about details translates into successful projects. But Lydia is such a perfectionist that, when handed a new assignment, she tends to immediately start fretting about the best way to start. Her boss told me that Lydia didn't appear sure about her plans because of her worried demeanor. People hesitated to follow her directions because she often looked so anxious and uncertain.

Lydia understood that she'd be a better leader if she could appear more decisive. To work on this, she explored various forms of "self-talk" before settling on two techniques. First, before entering a meeting, she would define her intent for the occasion. It might be something such as, "I'm going to raise point X and come across as interested and positive." Then she'd encourage herself with repeated affirmations such as, "My plan is on target and I know it will work."

Lydia also became conscious of her body language, and realized that when anxious she'd bow her head, cross her arms, and hunch her shoulders. Inspired by Dr. Cuddy's moving TED Talk, "Your Body Language Shapes Who You Are," she began practicing "power posing." Before making a presentation or attending an important event, she would go through a quick series of exercises, like holding her arms up high in a V shape. She said that the poses did seem to make her feel surer of herself. She also started regular yoga classes again and found that they helped her body stop feeling—and looking—so tense.

I spoke with Lydia's boss a few months after she began working on her presence and he was surprised by her transformation in such a short time.

Building presence can mean work on many levels

There is much you can do to rapidly enhance your executive presence. And, on a deeper level, you can continue to strengthen your presence through exercises intended to develop the level of your self-awareness. *Use these questions to check in with four aspects of yourself:*

1) **Your physical self:**

   ◆ How is my posture? Am I tense? Shall I relax my shoulders and other parts of my body?

   ◆ What is the expression on my face? Am I frowning? Is my jaw clenched? Can I generate a smile?

   ◆ How is my breathing? Is it shallow or hurried? Is it time for a deep, slow breath?

2) **Your intellectual self:**

   ◆ Has that internal voice been nagging me with worries and regrets? Shall I put them aside for now?

   ◆ What are my top goals for the day? For the next hour?

   ◆ What is my plan for reaching my most immediate goal?

   ◆ Is it time to shift my focus away from my own problems and onto another person?

3) **Your emotional self:**

   ◆ Has there been a moment today when I experienced an intense emotion? What was it?

   ◆ Did that surge of emotion impact the way I responded to another person?

   ◆ What am I feeling now?

   ◆ Are there feelings I want to let go, before going back to work?

4) **Your spiritual self:**

   ◆ What key values will help me with the decisions I must make today?

   ◆ Have my activities so far today been in keeping with the values that matter the most to me?

   ◆ What are three things I feel grateful for?

   ◆ Is it time for a moment of meditation, affirmation, or a quick prayer?

   ◆ Can I help someone?

17

To Make a Career Shift, Start with One Grain of Sugar

We all go through puzzling or difficult times. And sometimes we need a major change, perhaps even a new professional direction. You're the boss of your career. So when it's time to go another direction, you're the one who must come up with a plan.

But what do you do when you don't know where you want to go? There's no simple solution. Typically, what you must do is launch a process that sets the groundwork for your transition. From years of coaching experience, I know that the difference between just dreaming about a new phase, and actually getting there, often comes from setting up a methodical process that helps you to create change a little bit at a time.

Create your change process

Whether you want to shift professional tracks or simply pump up your performance in your current gig, setting up a change process that works for you will provide a clear starting point. When working with clients, I often suggest a technique for managing change that I've been using since I was a teenager.

When I was growing up, I followed my New Zealander parents' example and drank lots of tea. I liked it loaded with milk and sugar, but as a young teen I started worrying about the calories. I didn't want to give up my habit of drinking cups of tea every day after school, but kicking my sugar habit seemed too tough.

Then one day I was inspired to reduce the sugar so gradually that I'd never miss it. As I sat at the kitchen table, staring at the heaping pile of sugar on my spoon, I decided to make progress by removing just a few granules. In the following days, I estimated earlier volumes and tried to remove a few more grains. I kept at it, progressively lessening the amount of sugar from two or three spoonfuls to none. It took nearly a year, but I learned to enjoy sugarless tea without ever feeling deprived.

I was so intrigued by the power of creating change through small, painless steps that I applied what I called "the Sugar Grain Principle" to other aspects of my young life. For example, I became better at keeping my room neat with very small steps, like routinely shutting the closet door or spending just five minutes cleaning each morning.

I remembered the Sugar Grain Principle years later, as a senior at Ohio University. An injustice in the way female students were treated motivated me to support gender equality. I didn't expect to actually change practices that were widespread, but I thought the Principle might help to frame a satisfying gesture, just for me.

I promised myself to do at least one small "thing" in support of greater equality for university women every day. It didn't have to be much. A "thing" could be as small as a sugar grain. But I needed to come up with something—anything—every single day.

It was easy at first. A day's contribution might be as basic as speaking in class about equality. But with time it became more difficult to find my daily "thing," and I was forced to move out of my comfort zone. To meet my quota of sugar grains, I spoke at meetings, started a radio program focused on gender equality, and became the first woman to enter the university's MBA program.

As I scrambled harder to define new "things," I worried less about failure and became more creative. Eventually, the president noticed, made me his assistant, and asked me to write a detailed report on the status of women. Most of the report's recommendations were accepted, and ultimately I led

Ohio University's implementation of Title IX, the landmark federal legislation outlawing gender discrimination in education. I knew nothing about institutional change, but I found my way one sugar grain at a time.

In my job, I met individually with scores of women, often encouraging them to embark on career paths traditionally dominated by men. Still in my 20s, I was called upon to advise faculty members, and others far more experienced than I, who wanted to step into leadership or into fields traditionally closed to women.

I had no training in career development. Once again, I relied on my experience with gradual change. I developed a model that, at least inside my head, I called the "Sugar Grain Process." I used the model to help professionals rethink their goals and start taking steps in new directions.

Through the years I've repeatedly worked through the Sugar Grain Process while navigating my own varied career. And I've shared the process countless times, as a mentor, a manager, and coach.

I understand that the Sugar Grain Process is not unique and that many similar models can create success. But I have 40 years of experience in fostering career change using this approach, and I am absolutely confident that it works.

How to change careers with the Sugar Grain Process

Let's say you're bored with the kind of work you've been doing, but you don't know what you'd like to do next. *If I were your coach, I'd suggest you go through this five-part process:*

1) **Develop a vision of the career you want.** Your "vision" is a wish list of elements you'd like to see in your next career phase. Don't worry if you can't be precise. Chances are you will be surprised at how much you already know.

    ◆   **Start your list with pros and cons of your current position.** First on your list are the things you appreciate about your job—elements that you hope will continue. Then consider the negatives: Does each "con" suggest an opposite "pro" that belongs on your wish list? For example, if you don't like the isolation brought by your current project, you might add a "pro," like "more frequent social interaction," to your list.

- ◆ **Jump ahead and look back.** Imagine it's three years from now, and the past three years were professionally satisfying. Envision yourself feeling very successful. Now describe what made the past three-year period so productive and satisfying. What did you do, or what occurred to bring you to this good place? Maybe, in this imagined future, you met a new group of people or built your profile on social media? Does this exercise suggest elements you want to add to your vision list?

- ◆ **Consider elements you want in your life.** Ask yourself whether the worst part of your job is what it's doing to the rest of your life. Should your wish list include time or opportunities to pursue interests or relationships that would make your life more meaningful? For example, if what you really want is to spend more time with your kids, maybe "less weekend work" should go on your career wish list. Or perhaps you want to live in a different kind of place?

2) **State your most pressing goals.** After studying your wish list, define several achievable goals that could pave the way for your shift. For many people, three is a good number of goals for getting started. And these initial goals don't have to be precise. You might start with something like: (1) broaden my professional network; (2) learn to better manage stress; and (3) develop expertise in an important technical area.

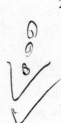

3) **Identify some "Sugar Grains" for each goal.** Once you have identified goals, even if they're not yet specific, it's time to start finding little things—the Sugar Grains—that will move you roughly in the direction that you want to go. Start a list of Grains—small action items—for each goal. For example, your Grains on stress might include taking a meditation class and ordering a useful book. As you build out your list of future Grains, keep these points in mind:

- ◆ **It doesn't matter where you start.** I don't call these little items "steps" because they aren't linear. Sugar Grains don't need to take you in a logical order along a direct path. The Grains on your list needn't be related to one another. And sometimes they'll feel pretty random. What matters is that you start to build momentum by doing *something*. As you find more Grains, patterns will emerge and your goals will become clearer.

◆ **Grains vary widely.** Let's say one of your goals is to become more prominent in your professional circles. Your first Grains might include sending an e-mail to an old contact, attending an event you'd typically skip, spending one hour setting up your LinkedIn account, and buying a notebook to use for new writing projects. The more varied and imaginative your Grains are, the better.

◆ **Grains will lead to other Grains.** I love the way doing one little thing so often inspires something else. For example, if you attend a dinner where you meet somebody interesting, your next Grain could be to send a follow-up note.

4) **Commit to a specific pace of Sugar Grains.** Once you have a picture of where you want to go, decide how quickly you need to move. That will determine how many Grains you'll want to accomplish each day, or week, for each goal. For example, if you're starting the hunt for a different sort of job, but you're not in a hurry, maybe you'll promise yourself to do just one thing each week. But it's vital to set a pace and maintain it, no matter what. *This is important: The power of the Sugar Grain Process comes from your commitment to keep up your pace even when you feel like you are out of ideas or don't have the time.*

5) **Maintain records.** Keeping track of your Grains helps ensure the success of your process. Your recordkeeping will help you see your progress, bring you new insights, and inspire additional Grains. How you do it, whether it's on paper or in the Cloud, is your choice. In addition to holding onto your lists of completed things, consider using logs for tracking your activity. For example, whether you're making notes on your calendar or maintaining an Excel spreadsheet, you're more likely to stick to an exercise or other program if you record each minute you spend. Another valuable tool can be your journal. Writing about your efforts promotes self-reflection, helps you explore and keep track of new ideas, and gives you a way to manage frustration and setbacks in the course of your transition.

As with any change effort, the most difficult part of the Sugar Grain Process can be getting started. But once you build up a cadence of Grains, the Process generates its own energy. You'll start to trust it and feel sure that it's taking you somewhere interesting and important. You'll probably go through several iterations, tweaking your goals as you move closer to your destination. Then, like many of my clients, you may hear yourself saying, "I'll kind of miss the Sugar Grain Process. It was getting to be fun."

18

How to Take a Career Side Step, One Sugar Grain at a Time

In the last chapter I wrote about the "Sugar Grain Process," the approach I use to create change in my career, as well as to guide mentees and clients. The essential idea is develop a vision of what you want next, and then commit to regularly doing little things that will move you in that direction. The things you do needn't be big—they can be as small as grains of sugar—but if you keep doing them at a regular pace, the process inevitably brings positive change.

A while back I received an e-mail from Susan*, a reader whom I've not met. She described herself as a woman in her 50s who wants to find a different kind of job, while remaining in the same broad career field.

"I am physically fit and healthy, and plan on working eight to 10 more years. I want to get out of [this] environment, have a different set of responsibilities, and make more money. Can you advise me?" Susan asked.

Well, that was a big question. And if Susan were a coaching client I'd start by asking her lots of questions in return. However, because an investment in coaching doesn't seem to be an option for Susan, I told her I'd take up the challenge of laying out a plan that could lead to her new job.

If you want to stay in your field, but find a different kind of job, get started one Sugar Grain at a Time

Susan had no idea how to start her search for a different kind of job within her industry. *I applied the Sugar Grain Process and came up with this plan for launching her transition:*

1) **Write a big wish list.** Start by listing everything you want in your next phase. Dream about what would be great not only in your job, but also in the rest of your life. Sometimes we start wishing for a career shift, but part of what we want may be available without a job change. For example, if you're bored or lonely, you might create a richer life by pursuing new interests in your free time. Or, if you love your job but want more income, you might consider creating a side business.

2) **Organize your wish list.** Break your list into categories within your new life. Think broadly, and include headings like "health and fitness" or "social life," as well as "ideal job attributes." You are creating this larger vision partly because it will help you to see that not everything must be found through your work. But there may be exciting career benefits, as well, because creating positive change in *any* part of your life can bring new energy to your job. I often see that when clients make progress in one area, like their fitness program or their volunteer activity, it resonates in their work lives.

3) **Commit to regular cadence of Sugar Grains.** Once you have your categories, start moving by doing little things—the tiny Grains—to support each one. Decide how many Grains you'll undertake each week for each category. It's important to find a realistic pace, and then stick with it faithfully. For example, you might decide that each week for the first two months you will:

♦ **Support your job search** with three Grains. The first week might include (1) e-mailing to arrange a lunch date with a professional contact, (2) spending 20 minutes doing research on the Internet, and (3) working on your resume for 30 minutes.

♦ **Start exercising** by walking for 20 minutes three times during the week.

♦ **Take one social step,** like making a phone call to arrange a future dinner with friends.

4) **Do research and notice trends.** While you've been busy in your day job, you may not have been tracking developments in your professional area. Your job-related Grains should include looking around, identifying people who are making contributions, money, or headlines. Read everything you can, but don't stop there. Look for conferences and associations where you can learn from people working in fields not far removed from yours.

5) **Network methodically.** On your list of potential Grains will be the names of people who might be willing to brainstorm with you. Include not only those you've known well through the years, but also professional acquaintances who seem career savvy. Then work your list. Set up coffee dates, or find other ways to visit with just about anybody who might be able to spot trends or suggest opportunities. Ask your contacts if they can suggest others who might be willing to talk with you. If people are too busy to help, they'll let you know. And, if they are willing to chat, know that someday you'll be able to return the favor or pay it forward with another job seeker.

6) **Engage online.** Social media is now playing a major role in the job search arena. Today's job seekers are at a disadvantage if they don't at least have profiles on LinkedIn.com. Twitter is also a tool that allows you to connect with recruiters and others you might not be able to reach by phone or e-mail.

7) **Learn something new.** Taking classes is an excellent way to pick up new skills and broaden your perspective. When you are engaged in learning, it helps you see your routine work in new ways and become more creative. And certifications earned

through course work can demonstrate your commitment to excellence. Enrolling in classes at a local college could have the additional benefit of broadening your network. But if there's no nearby option, explore distance learning.

8) **Volunteer.** If you want to build additional skills, look for ways to get new kinds of experience. A good starting point can be to join clubs or service organizations.

9) **Find a buddy.** Making a career shift can be a lonely process. Find a friend who is also engaged in reinvention and meet regularly to share ideas, networks, and encouragement. You don't have to have similar careers. Somebody in a different line of work might offer a new way of looking at things.

I never heard back from Susan, but I've shared this plan with other readers, and more than one has reported good results.

16/10

19

Those Annoying Speech Habits May Cost You

Innovation often flows from collaboration among people who have different views, backgrounds, and skill sets. Varied teams are more likely to come up with something new than a group of professionals with similar backgrounds. When people are able to get along, diversity can give rise to startling creativity. And it can be deeply satisfying when you're part of a diverse team that clicks along.

But it's not always easy to fit within a mixed team. One thing that can hold you back is a conversational style that other members find annoying.

Here's a game to build awareness among members of the older set

In today's workplace, one way that managers are learning to foster fresh thinking is by partnering 45-and-older expert professionals with younger and more

tech, and social media-savvy colleagues. Work teams cutting across generations have so much potential that it's a shame the trend isn't building even
faster. However, one barrier to cooperation across the decades is that people of
different ages sometimes communicate in dissimilar ways.

Let's face it: At times Baby Boomers and Millennials find each other's
conversation to be boring. Ageism seems to be on the rise, and at work the
communication gap may have the most serious consequences for the Boomers.
People who are older than the group average can lose professional credibility
if they indulge in tedious conversational patterns, whether they're speaking in
meetings or during a casual lunch. And if their coworkers see them as out of
date, they could be excluded from the most interesting projects.

Recently, a group of Boomer friends were talking about the tedious
chatter of our age cohort. In particular, we all confessed to occasionally
indulging in prolonged accounts of our various aches and pains. We bore
even each other with this kind of talk and could drive a younger colleague
out of the room.

So we invented "Code Blue," a game that allows us to remind each other
to avoid annoying old person talk. The goal of the game is to gently cue friends
to change gears when their speech is falling into a geezer pattern. The primary
rule is that reminders must be offered in a spirit of kindness, and only to willing players.

***To play the game, when the occasion arises, you quietly mention one
of three applicable warning codes:***

→ **Code Blue** (for blue hair) is our signal to end a stream of complaints about the speaker's less than perfect physical condition.
   I'm not talking about interrupting a serious talk about health
   challenges with a dear friend. Rather, the idea is to help each
   other resist the temptation to complain about our sore backs in
   any setting where the conversation would be better focused on
   something else. If you want to play, empower your colleague or
   partner to give you a gentle "Code Blue" reminder should you
   start to rant about the state of your body.

→ **Code Green** is a signal I invented while eavesdropping on the
   next table at a local bistro. There, a prosperous looking young
   couple was buying dinner for the man's mother, a woman in
   her 60s or older. Instead of expressing appreciation for the great
   choices, Mom embarrassed her son by going through the menu
   loudly complaining about the current cost of restaurant food.

When the waiter took her order, she said, "Well, what I really want is the swordfish, but I'd never let him pay that much, so bring me the pasta." The son seemed mortified and adjoining diners were rolling their eyes. This can happen in many different discussions about how much things cost today, including in a business context. So when your office pal once again wastes time with the discovery that prices have gone up since 1995, offer the gentle reminder: "Code Green."

→ **Code Golden Harvest** is used when people interrupt a discussion about a current topic with yet another story of what it was like back in the day. "Golden Harvest" was a wildly popular color for appliances and décor from the 60s into the 80s. But there's a reason people stopped using that shade and we're all still tired of it. If you're frequently tempted to reminisce when future thinking is what's needed, let your closest colleague know that it's okay to sometimes whisper "Code Golden Harvest."

Be aware of your speech habits, whatever your age

Older people aren't the only ones in danger of undercutting their professional brands with annoying talk. Individuals of all ages may make themselves unpopular by speaking way too much about topics not of interest to their audience. And even individuals with interesting content can muddle their messages with tedious or confusing speech patterns.

Recent college graduates can sometimes drive coworkers to distraction with "up-talking." You're an up-talker if you tend to end your statements with upward inflections, making them sound like questions. It's a babyish habit that can change the meaning of a sentence and make you sound timid.

We must add to the list of poor communicators anyone who indulges in too much profanity within a culture that values polite speech. And then there are the whiners—they'll never make it into the inner circle of a team that values a positive attitude. Finally, if you, uh, break up your, ah, sentences with, y'know, too many little, um, tics, your points may not be heard.

We tend not to notice our own speech patterns and may not be aware when they're interfering with our ability to be clear or connect with others. If you have doubts about how your talking comes across, ask friends to listen to you carefully and report on what they hear. Or record your next speech. Find a way to explore questions like these:

→ Do I use the same words or phrases—like, "Awesome" or "Am I right?"—over and over?

→ Is there anything about my tone that seems grating or difficult to make out?

→ Do I take too long to make my point, sometimes arguing my case even after I've won?

→ Do I speak so fast that some people may have trouble understanding?

→ Do I weaken the impact of my points with tentative preliminary phrasing like, "I'm not sure, but I think that . . ."

→ Do I constantly say "I" no matter what topic is under discussion?

If other people are bored, annoyed, or confused by the way you talk, they may tune you out. Make an effort to be aware of your speech habits, and be clear about the conversational style you'd like to have as part of your personal brand.

20

Does Your Calendar Support Your Success?

Do you feel overwhelmed by having too much to do in too little time? If you want to accomplish more without spending longer at your desk or laptop, you may need a better way to manage your schedule. But it's difficult to rethink how you keep your calendar if everything just feels like a blur.

To revise the way you manage your calendar, begin with an assessment of exactly what you're doing with all those hours at work. To get a more accurate look at how you're employing your time, keep a detailed log for a week or two. Throughout each day, record what you do and how many minutes you spend on each activity. When you study your log, you may be surprised by how much of each week is devoted to things that don't really matter.

Once you have a better handle on where your time is going, you can make adjustments to help you become more productive. Your calendar can become a more powerful tool for keeping you focused on your highest priorities and making good use of your energy, as well as your time.

These strategies can help you rethink your calendar

My client Gina* is a successful executive who earns more money, and makes bigger decisions, than she ever dreamed possible. From "360 review" interviews with several of her colleagues and clients, I know that she is widely seen as energetic, compassionate, and very smart.

But Gina came to coaching because she felt like her work life was out of control. She was spending long hours at the office, but she didn't feel efficient and her backlog of work was growing. She often arrived late to meetings and worried constantly about forgetting something important. And she was troubled by a sense that she didn't have time to focus on the big challenges she saw down the road for her team.

I asked Gina to take careful notes, for just two weeks, of how she actually employed her time in the office. As she reviewed her carefully kept log, she was startled by the true picture of her work patterns. She saw that she spent way too much time on low-value e-mail, and she let herself be frequently hijacked from her planned activities. She'd long been proud of her open door policy and reputation as a responsive colleague. But when she looked at how frequently she was interrupted, she understood the high cost. Gina was devoting relatively little attention to her most critical goals.

She decided that a key to becoming more efficient and less stressed would be to change the way she approached her calendar. To begin, we talked about how Gina's work life is shaped by a complex pattern of commitments. As each day goes along, she continues to make promises and enter into agreements. On a typical day she might say "yes" to several meetings, swear to make progress on a major project, and agree to review multiple drafts from anxious colleagues. She'd put the meetings on her calendar and maybe even block out time for her most pressing work. But then, all too often, her attention would be swept up by calls, visits from coworkers, and minor crises. She might go for hours without even glancing at her full calendar.

The log helped Gina see how frequently she missed deadlines because she was ignoring her calendar. And she had an "Aha!" moment. She realized that every time she was late or a no-show, another person might be inconvenienced or disappointed. She said, "I finally understood that one reason I felt so anxious is that I was going through life letting people down."

Gina decided to get serious about treating her calendar as a primary tool for managing both her time and her commitments. During a period of several months, she gradually rebuilt some work habits, learned new scheduling techniques, and found ways to focus more attention on her highest priorities. Once she rebuilt her relationship with her calendar, Gina felt more in control and much less stressed. *These scheduling tips were helpful to Gina and they may help you:*

→ **Take time to plan.** Look at your calendar first thing every morning and frequently throughout the day so that you can envision what lies ahead, complete necessary preparation for the next event, and spot any problems. Notice the gaps between appointments and decide in advance how to use that available time to accomplish your most pressing tasks.

→ **Coordinate with your "to-do" list.** As you look at your task list, batch similar kinds of action items, like phone calls or brief e-mails. Then schedule blocks of time to work through each batch. For example, if you have to make a lot of phone calls, schedule one-hour blocks for quickly getting through your call list.

→ **Match your calendar to your body clock.** Many people find that they are more efficient at some times of the day than at others. Gina knew that her mind is sharpest in the morning and that she often feels too tired to think clearly by late afternoon. But she saw from her log that she often spent her morning hours answering routine e-mail, visiting with colleagues, and handling relatively simple administrative tasks. She'd put off her most challenging and important work until the end of the day, often staying late into the night when she was too exhausted to think straight. So she reorganized her routine to dedicate more of her high-quality morning hours to her top projects. Several days a week she would close her door and ignore e-mail for a couple of hours. She said the new practice changed her life.

→ **Push for shorter meetings.** Would you have more time for your top projects if you didn't have to go to so many meetings? Chances are that some of your regular meetings take longer than they should. And if you're frustrated by the wasted time, other participants probably are as well. So even if you aren't chairperson, you may be able to convince your colleagues to experiment with quicker meetings. For example, if a meeting normally takes an hour, propose restructuring so that it lasts only 45 minutes.

→ **Resist distraction.** Once your plan for the day is in place, your next big challenge may be to avoid being hijacked by phone calls, e-mails, visitors, and your own compulsion to multitask. To be more efficient, you may need to overcome old habits, like checking e-mail every 10 minutes or answering the phone every time it rings. Your log will help you notice where your plans tend to go awry. Sometimes honoring your commitments means learning how to fight off other requests and temptations.

→ **Renegotiate your schedule as you go along.** The demands you face change constantly, and life does get in the way of your carefully planned agenda. Your goal is not to be a slave to your calendar, but rather to be impeccable in the way you use it to *manage* your commitments. When you're faced with the unexpected, you can often renegotiate dates and deadlines. Gina found life to be less stressful once she learned to anticipate scheduling problems and work out alternative plans.

→ **Align your time and priorities.** Your well-kept calendar can provide a clear picture of where your time goes. As you look at it, regularly ask whether the distribution of your time is consistent with your priorities. Is most of your time going to your most important activities? Are you saying "yes" to requests when your list of current objectives suggests that you should decline? And are you building in time for things that really matter to you personally, such as working out at the gym and other ways to take care of yourself? As you schedule, remember to honor not only the promises you make to other people, but also the commitments you make to yourself.

→ **Say "no."** A chunk of your day may be devoted to activities that feel urgent but aren't really very important. Maybe you agree to attend meetings or undertake projects not because they matter to you, but because you want to be nice, because you like to avoid conflict, or because "yes" is just your knee-jerk response. If so, you should probably get better at saying "no." And saying "no" gets easier with practice as you find ways to tactfully decline proposals and opportunities that aren't consistent with your priorities. One useful technique is to pause before you say "yes," in order to ask yourself what you'll give up if you don't say "no." For example, if a coworker invites you to a meeting that sounds kind of interesting, hesitate before saying "okay," and think about what else you could do with that hour.

21

Prioritize Your Priorities

In Chapter 20 we talked about how my client Gina developed better control of her work life by rethinking the way she approached her calendar. When Gina committed to more actively managing her schedule, one of her goals was to devote more of her work time to her most important activities. But when I asked Gina to name her highest priorities, she had a hard time deciding what should go on that list.

It is tempting to just react to whatever seems most pressing as a day goes along, and Gina often fell into that trap. She sometimes lost track of her more significant objectives because at any given moment they felt less urgent than other people's demands for action or attention.

Realizing she didn't have enough time or energy to go around, Gina resolved to think more carefully about how to flag high-value work. She decided that once a week she'd arrive early near her downtown office and spend an hour or so at her favorite coffee shop, sorting out her immediate priorities as she reviewed her calendar and project list. *Here is the seven-point system that Gina uses stay in touch with her priorities, and a similar approach might work for you:*

1) **Remember the big picture.** A good foundation for setting your priorities is to draft a list or statement about what matters most. Gina wrote a "career vision," which was basically a list of her key values and work-life goals. It included items like, "nurture my team members," "stay current in my field," and "have time for a rich social life." Gina keeps a copy of her vision with her calendar and looks at it during her weekly priority review session.

2) **Prioritize work categories.** Gina knew that the items on her lengthy task list weren't equally productive. But she tended to vacillate in gauging their importance. Her particular problem was that she was easily sidetracked by other people's sense of urgency. She decided to keep her assignments on a steady course by sorting activities into these four categories:

   Tier One: Important to her bosses, to their goals, and to their success.

   Tier Two: Important to the goals and the success of her direct reports.

   Tier Three: Related to her routine management responsibilities, like human resource and budget matters.

   Tier X: Stuff that could be done by other people.

3) **Create a daily "List of 3."** A technique that made a big difference in Gina's efficiency was her new practice of starting every morning with a list of three tasks that must be done by day's end. These are the items that are so useful or important that their completion may make the day a success, no matter what else happens. She writes the list on an index card and posts it where she'll see it frequently.

4) **Schedule time for high priorities.** Gina makes standing appointments with herself and blocks out time on her calendar for both her List of 3 and tasks related to her Tier One projects. Because she feels most productive in the morning, she often sets aside and closely guards a block of time between 10 o'clock and noon. On some days she'll use this precious time block to concentrate on a single project, and on others she'll spend the hours moving quickly through a number of small steps for a variety of important assignments.

5) **Schedule low value time for lower-value work.** Administrative and other routine tasks may be of lower priority than your major projects, but they still have to be completed in a timely way. Because Gina feels less efficient late in the day, she sets aside some afternoon hours for handling this kind of work. She often makes a game of it by seeing how fast she can speed through her list. And she rewards herself, sometimes by leaving a little early, when she completes certain tedious reports.

6) **Find the biggest bang for your buck.** Some things aren't top priority in the grand scheme of things, but they're worth doing immediately because of how much trouble they'll save you in the long run. For example, if you suspect that a quick explanatory meeting would allow you to calm down a disgruntled colleague, you might want to add it to your List of 3. If you wait, the problem may fester and ultimately the misunderstanding will require much more of your energy to resolve.

7) **Get rid of clutter.** Some activities on your "to-do" list or calendar just aren't of high enough priority to be worth doing. Yet they tend to linger on your list, sometimes distracting you or making you feel guilty. It can feel liberating to get real about your odds of finishing these low value action items. Gina now scrutinizes her calendar and task list for this kind of clutter and says it feels great to delete it.

Play with prioritization systems until you find one that works

Time management experts have written about many different ways for setting priorities. I tend to be cautious about recommending any single approach because I've found that the clients most likely to stick with a system are the ones, like Gina, who develop their own hybrid approaches.

What may be most important is that you regularly pause and evaluate the relative importance and urgency of all the things you feel you must do. *As you go through your evaluation process, ask yourself questions such as these:*

→ How would I rank the relative importance of these items?

→ How do they relate to this year's top performance objectives? To my most important long-term career goals?

→ Is this both urgent and important? Or just urgent?

→ What will happen if I don't get this done?

→ What does my boss or client want most from me?

→ What actions will assure that this is a productive day?

→ What will I learn from this? Will it help me to grow?

→ Will this help me build or improve relationships with other people?

→ Could this expand my business or job description?

→ What will it take to make this a success?

10 / 10 / 16

12 / " / 16

22

Getting Your Boss to Listen

How can I get the boss to listen?" That's a question I often hear from clients. Perhaps you have the same problem. Is it sometimes hard to complete a project because you can't get the boss's attention? Do you head home feeling frustrated because your boss won't give you the feedback you need? Or, even worse, does your career feel off-kilter because you and your leader are out of sync?

No boss is perfect, most managers are too busy, and some are flat out weak. But complaining won't get you anywhere, and you have too much at stake to just throw up your hands when the communication process breaks down.

Part of your strategy as an entrepreneurial professional is to communicate smoothly with your bosses and clients, no matter how difficult it may be to reach them. Your goal is to assure delivery of your key messages even when it doesn't seem fair that you have to do so much of the hard work.

These tips can help you get through to your boss

Even if you and your boss communicate pretty well, *these strategies can make your messages even more effective:*

1) **Be succinct.** Assume your boss is busy and won't want to waste time. If you ask for three minutes to discuss something important but then talk for 10 before reaching your point, the boss could be feeling impatient or annoyed by the time you make your case.

2) **Plan ahead.** Before your conversation, be clear in your mind about your points, and be prepared to state them simply and directly. To prevent confusion or distraction, limit the number of items you intend to raise. If you've requested a meeting where you'll discuss several issues, propose a brief written agenda. A simple e-mail with a sentence about each topic can set up your conversation in a good way.

3) **Be clear about your goal.** Sometimes you have to choose between having your say and having your way. It can be tempting to use your face time for venting about your problems, but that might not lead to solutions. Be strategic in the way you frame your issues, and focus on positive proposals that will support your specific objectives.

4) **Understand their communication preferences.** If you don't get through, it may not be the content of your message so much as how or when you deliver it. Different people take in and share information in different ways. For example, bosses who are extroverts may be "external processors" who want to use you as a sounding board while they explore their own thoughts. While in processing mode they might not pay much attention to your agenda, so you should wait. And introverts may find listening to be tiring, so don't make your pitch after they've been through exhausting meetings. Notice how your boss communicates with her boss or clients, and try the same techniques. If she tends to put her most important requests in writing, do the same with yours.

5) **Be a mindful listener.** Strong communicators are active listeners. Your bosses expect you to listen carefully, and good listening helps you understand what they want. But at times when we think we're listening, we're sometimes focused on something else, such as what we want to say next. When you truly concentrate on deep listening, you'll come across to your boss as alert, centered, and respectful.

6) **Let go of frustration.** If the boss doesn't seem to listen, you actually have two challenges. The first, of course, is to break through the logjam by becoming an even better communicator. But there is only so much you can do, and much of this is about the boss, not about you. So the next challenge is to learn how to not let it bother you so much. It's vital that you don't obsess, or your annoyance could make the situation worse. Writing in a journal is one way to examine your negative reactions and let go of some of the emotion.

23

Leading Upward: Manage the Boss, in a Good Way

Although successful leadership styles vary considerably, the best leaders have attributes in common. For example, most tend to have integrity, strong value systems, and a genuine desire to do the right thing. The leaders I most admire are consistently willing to step forward and serve, even if a task is menial or unlikely to lead to recognition. And their influence over other people extends in all directions. In other words, not only are they adept at managing their direct reports, but they are also able to guide other colleagues and collaborators.

Some of the stronger leaders exercise a special skill. They are able to lead upward, influencing their bosses to make better decisions and become more effective. For example, there's Sam*, who didn't expect to rise beyond his role as the VP of communications. He had five years until retirement, and he wanted during that time to contribute even more to the company he loved.

Without telling his colleagues, Sam adopted the goal of thoroughly supporting and even mentoring Joe, his young and recently arrived CEO. Because of his job, Sam had a good, comprehensive view of the company's activities and customer relationships. And he made an effort to listen to colleagues and stakeholders at every level. Sam gathered and sorted feedback and data, and relayed it in a positive, effective way to Joe. Being well informed, and having Sam as a sounding board, helped Joe to grow quickly into his job. And his private mission of fully supporting Joe made Sam's last years of work more interesting and rewarding.

In my own corporate career, the boss who taught me most about leadership was a humble guy named Dave Weatherwax. During his decade as senior VP and general counsel of Consolidated Natural Gas Company, Dave remained modest and never seemed to seek the limelight. And yet he exercised great influence, often quietly guiding the rest of the C-Suite.

During my first year with the CNG, I watched Dave carefully, trying to learn from his low-key but effective approach to management. Finally the day came when a colleague and I met with Dave to pitch a major initiative, asking his support for a public outreach project we thought might be outside his comfort zone. In making our case, I raised every argument I could think of, carefully framing my points to reflect Dave's goals, interests, and possible concerns.

Dave listened intently, and then to our surprise he approved the proposal on the spot. His only change was to set a budget much bigger than the one we'd requested. We were almost giddy with success as we left his office. Then he stuck his head out his door and called us back. He said, "I just want you to know that I saw what you were doing. But I don't mind being led, if it's done really well."

Dave let us know that upward management can benefit everyone, but it must be done adroitly and in the right spirit. ***Here are strategies to consider if you want to become better at leading up:***

→ **First, set unselfish goals.** Leading upward is not the same
    thing as trying to manipulate the situation so you look good
    or somehow score a win. "Leading" is about offering proposals,
    guidance, and support that serve the interests of the organiza-
    tion. When you step in to lead your boss, your intent should be
    to remain relatively invisible as you give the enterprise a helpful
    nudge. You quietly act like a CEO, serving the team with vision
    and integrity, and nobody else needs to know about it. Part of

Dave's leadership strength was his authentic humility. He had no interest in self-aggrandizement, but sincerely cared about serving the greater good.

→ **Understand what your bosses need.** If you want to influence and assist the people above you, it's critical to have a good sense of their goals and responsibilities. Develop a theory of how success will look from their perspective. Consider the organization's mission, current strategy, and primary challenges, and look carefully at what your bosses are trying to accomplish.

→ **Maintain your areas of expertise.** One reason for Dave's considerable influence was that everybody respected his judgment as a lawyer. Even after his portfolio was broadened to include a variety of functions, he was recognized as the ultimate legal expert. A good way to maximize your influence is to develop an area where you are recognized as *the* authority. Find a niche where you can excel and bring value to the enterprise by remaining current and by continuing to build your special skills and knowledge.

→ **Be gracious in managing credit and blame.** Dave understood that credit is a vast resource to be spread around, not hoarded. He worked hard to make his boss, the CEO, look good. And when things were going well in his area, he invited his team to step forward and be thanked for the good work. Though Dave was lavish in sharing credit, he didn't indulge in spreading blame. When problems arose, he took responsibility. When someone made a mistake, he typically examined the situation in a lawyer-like way, and then turned immediately to finding solutions.

→ **Report without drama.** Your boss is more likely to rely on you if she can count on you to report the facts in a simple, straightforward way. Create a strong network for gathering information and build your credibility by telling the truth without indulging in gossip, exaggeration, or negative commentary. It makes sense to be tactful, but you won't be acting like a leader if you only tell your boss what she wants to hear.

→ **Be organized.** Your bosses' time is limited, and one way you can assist them is by making sure that none of it is wasted.

When you meet with them, be prompt, stick with an agenda, and don't talk any longer than necessary. Look for opportunities to help your bosses keep things moving smoothly and find ways to save them from unnecessary stress.

A good approach for improving your upward management skills is to search for role models. Look around for people who are successful in leading upward, and learn from how they do it. And, if you already head a team, watch for times when one of the members is particularly skillful at managing *you*. Notice whether they are good at leading up because they save you time, provide you with something you need, or make you feel more positive.

24

The Jimmy Fallon Touch: Good Manners Help You Shine

I was delighted when a radio commentator reported that the National League of Junior Cotillions chose Jimmy Fallon to top its "Best-Mannered List for 2014."

According to the League's Website, Fallon was selected as Number One "for maintaining the dignity and respect of others through his comedic disposition as host of *The Tonight Show*."

I can't think of a better choice. Part of what makes Fallon so charming is that he invariably seems delighted to be with his guests and determined to help them look good. Much of our enjoyment comes from his intense interest in their success and his whole body laughter at their jokes. Even if you don't think he's funny, you can't help but like Jimmy Fallon. Perhaps social graces like his are so appealing because they are a low-key application of the Golden Rule. The way he interacts with others seems to say: I'll be nice to you and I have confidence that you'll be nice to me.

The ideals of polite behavior may not be a topic of discussion in your workplace. But you'll know what your colleague means if he describes someone as "a real gentleman," or "a true lady." People with excellent social manners tend to stand out. And we enjoy being with polite people because they tend to notice us and are so aware of *our* needs.

For a personal brand that sets you apart from the crowd, learn from Fallon. Develop a reputation for treating everyone with respect. Of course, what counts most are the big things, like pitching in to support your coworkers in a crisis. But you can enhance your brand by consistently exhibiting good manners in even small ways. *These seven strategies can help you develop the Jimmy Fallon touch:*

1) **Say "hello."** When we're around other people, it's always decent to acknowledge their presence. Your rude coworkers may act like others are invisible, but with a simple "good morning" you can forge a sense of connection and goodwill.

2) **Shake hands.** The perfect handshake is valued in U.S. culture, and it allows you to exude confidence and warmth. This simple gesture can help you to make a good first impression, reconnect with someone you haven't seen in a while, or say a polished "goodbye." Try these tips to perfect your handshake:

   - Be quick to extend your right hand, particularly if you are the older person or have the higher authority.

   - Look the other person in the eye before and during your handshake. And offer a greeting or pleasantry such as, "It's great to meet you."

   - Allow your grip to be firm but not crushing.

   - Shake your hand up and down, just a few inches, and not more than once or twice.

3) **Speak with basic courtesy.** Your habits of speech say a lot about you. These guidelines set a minimum standard:

   - Be quick to say "please" and "thank you" to everyone.

   - Say "excuse me" if you bump into or must interrupt someone.

   - Avoid profanity and crude language.

   - Praise or congratulate folks on their achievements, even if it requires you to bite back a twinge of envy.

4) **Be considerate of others' time.** When people are busy, it's unkind to waste their minutes and hours:

- Be punctual for meetings and appointments.

- Respond quickly to invitations (to save time spent on follow-up).

- Don't waste time with rants or lengthy accounts of small matters.

- Don't play with your phone during a meeting or conversation.

5) **Treat colleagues with class.** The way you talk about others can shape your reputation:

- Don't gossip with coworkers about coworkers.

- Don't bad-mouth your boss, your team, or your organization.

- Share credit, paying special attention to junior team members whose work might otherwise go unnoticed.

6) **Debate with civility.** Disagreement is part of the creative process and responsible professionals aren't afraid to speak up, but that's no excuse for being mean:

- Express criticism in terms of the work or the concept, and avoid making it about the person.

- When possible, frame your comments in a positive way.

- Avoid sarcasm because it's seldom amusing and can lead to misunderstandings.

- Let the other side speak, genuinely listen to their views, and imagine what it's like from their perspective.

7) **Dine with style.** Table manners are about assuring that everyone has a good time and nobody's enjoyment is ruined by someone else's gross behavior. Don't get hung up on questions about which fork to use. The point of standardized silverware rules is to make guests comfortable as they select the implement for each course. And nobody will care if you pick up the "wrong" fork. On the other hand, avoid disrupting the table by knowing which wine glass and bread plate belong to you. The standard is that

all glasses are placed on the right side of the main dinner plate ("drink to the right"), and other dishes are on the left ("eat to the left"). Beyond that, in U.S. business circles, these rules are widely accepted:

♦ Don't object when your host indicates where you should sit.

♦ Always chew with your mouth closed.

♦ Don't speak when you have food in your mouth.

♦ Eat quietly, taking small manageable bites.

♦ Don't slurp or blow on your food to cool it—just wait until it's not so hot.

♦ Never blow your nose on your napkin.

♦ Never pick your teeth at the table.

The main point is that people with the Jimmy Fallon touch project the message that everyone matters. They're considerate. And they help build cultures where everyone can collaborate, perform well, and enjoy the work. It's no wonder that other people like being around them.

25

Do's and Don'ts of Saying "Sorry"

As we discussed in Chapter 19, people often judge you by the way you speak. If you develop annoying speech mannerisms, distracted listeners may not value your comments or perceive the full scope of your expertise. On the other hand, your personal brand is enhanced when you're seen as someone who always seems to say the right thing.

Do you aspire to be one of those tactful, well-spoken people who are welcomed into most conversations? One way to begin to speak more gracefully is to listen carefully, so you can pick up cues from the crowd and adopt the best tone. Listening to the way other people interact enhances your sense of balance; it helps you to avoid the extremes of expressing too much or too little, or coming off as too warm or too cold.

Tact also requires an awareness of the tremendous power of certain words. Some words have more consequences than others and should be used with care. One of those big impact words is "sorry." It's typically defined to include emotions like regret, sadness, and penitence. But in practice it can have many shades of meaning. And when we say the phrase "I'm sorry" in a work environment, we might be expressing anything from remorse to subservience, uncertainty, or defiance.

The nuances of the word do vary with organizational cultures. ***But here's my take on how, when, and whether to say, "Sorry":***

→ **Do say you're sorry when you've done something wrong.** When you screw up on the job, the best plan is to confess immediately, apologize sincerely, and turn quickly to rectifying the situation or making sure it won't happen again. For the victim, when you say "mea culpa" you make a bit of moral restitution. Your discomfort gives him some power over you, and he is able to decide whether to accept your apology or to withhold forgiveness. But apologizing can benefit you, as well. When you 'fess up, it's like a reset button, giving you a chance to move on and restore the normal order.

→ **Be sincere.** Not all apologies improve matters. Your "sorry" is more likely to be favorably received when you mean it. You can transmit the intensity of your regret by describing how you actually feel ("I was so upset that I couldn't sleep last night") and proposing a way to make up for your wrongdoing.

→ **Do say "sorry" even if you weren't to blame.** Sometimes we say "I'm sorry" not to express remorse, but to show our compassion. This might happen when things go wrong in some way far beyond your control, such as when horrible weather inconveniences your guests. Or you might say "I'm so sorry" to acknowledge a personal loss, such as a death in the family. Some psychological research suggests that this kind of "superfluous" apology can promote a sense of trust and connection between you and the listener, and make everybody feel better.

→ **Don't say it when you don't mean it.** Saying "I'm sorry" when you actually feel the opposite can come across to the recipient like an insult. "Sorry" is a complex word and it can be inflammatory when your nonverbal message is the opposite of regret. Don't make the situation worse by accompanying the phrase "I'm sorry" with a grimace or an eye roll. And avoid beginning your sentence with "I'm sorry, *but* . . ." When you don't feel at fault, avoid making a fake apology. Instead, focus on improving the situation and say something positive such as, "Let's see what we can do to fix this."

→ **Don't say "sorry" to soften an insult.** If you say, "Sorry, but this draft is no good," don't think your wording will make the message any easier to accept. If your remorse is genuine, make clear what it is you regret and then be direct in the way you deliver the rest of the message. You might say, "I'm truly sorry if this will ruin your weekend, but the client needs a number of changes in your draft."

→ **Don't say "sorry" when there's nothing to apologize for.** Some people repeatedly say "sorry" as a conscious way to express deference or humility. For others, the pattern may be an unconscious expression of uncertainty. Either way, constant apologies can make you look frightened or powerless. My competent and generally confident client Tina* developed the verbal tic of saying "I'm sorry" every time she was about to ask a question or make a suggestion. Her use of the phrase became so engrained she didn't know she was saying it. As soon as this habit was brought to her attention, Tina realized it made her sound like she was experiencing a crisis of confidence. Her closest colleagues admitted they found it annoying and, with her permission, they helped Tina break the habit by reminding her when there was no need to apologize.

Do you think that you say "I'm sorry" too often? Or perhaps you find it difficult to apologize and don't do it often enough? Becoming more aware of your speech patterns can help you decide whether they need some tweaking. To capture a clear picture of this kind of speech habit, keep a log for a few weeks. Write down every instance in which you apologized, noting what you were regretting and any impact from your remark. Sometimes it's hard to hear your own words, so this could be an occasion to call upon friends to gently point out your habit.

26

Find the Magic 20 Percent

My most vivid memories of business school include a few instances when professor Bill Day put aside the class syllabus and spoke vividly about phenomena that could make a difference in our lives.

In one such discussion, the professor urged us to stay focused on the important things in life by relying on the 80/20 Rule. That rule of thumb tells us that most of the results in any situation are determined by a small number of the causes. Expressed another way, the Rule predicts that about 80 percent of your achievements will flow from about 20 percent of the things you do. The numbers of "80" and "20" aren't absolute. The key point is that your bottom line isn't impacted in the same amount by each unit of your work or of your time. So a small proportion of your activity may be responsible for most of what you get done.

The Rule seems to have endless applications and has been given a variety of names, like the "Law of the Vital Few." Many accounts suggest that it was first applied as a business principle about a century ago as "Pareto's Law." Economist Vilfredo Pareto wrote that, in any situation, just a small portion of the resources will yield most of the outputs. For example, he said that if a government were to give a number of poor people money to invest in small businesses, the investors wouldn't all be equally successful. A small group (the 20 percent) would make most of the money resulting from the investments (the 80 percent).

What captured my imagination was when Professor Day told us that computer modeling can illustrate principles, like the 80/20 Rule, that demonstrate how the universe isn't just hopeless disorder. It was comforting to hear his evidence that the world operates according to some kind of logic. And I welcomed his suggestion that we can spot familiar patterns and use them to make better choices in our careers and in life.

It isn't necessary to understand *why* it works. ***If you look around, you'll see numerous applications of the 80/20 Rule:***

→ In a big organization, a few of the managers may deliver the lion's share of results.

→ Of your many clients, only a few may account for most of your income.

→ If you offer multiple products, it's likely that several will deliver most of your profits.

→ If you have lots of customers, about 20 percent of them may voice about 80 percent of the complaints.

And the Rule probably holds true in your personal life:

→ Of all the things you do, a few bring you most of the fun.

→ Of all your skills, a few deliver most of the rewards.

→ Of the many people you know, a few are responsible for much of the joy.

With these strategies, the 80/20 Rule can help sharpen your career

The Rule can remind you to stop obsessing about the lower priorities on your "to-do" list and shift your attention to your major objectives. It can help you find a place to get started when you're feeling overwhelmed. It suggests that you consider which 20 percent of your workload may make the most difference, and stop worrying about all the rest that won't count so much.

When you're in doubt about what to do next, turn to the 80/20 Rule for guidance like this:

→ **Focus on the big goal.** Don't try to pursue every opportunity that comes along. When there's too much to do, concentrate on activities most directly related to your key objectives. Shift more of your attention to the 20-or-so percent of tasks or events most likely to support your top priorities.

→ **Don't try to be great at everything.** Find ways to spend more of your time on the activities that you do well and that yield results. Let's say you're a fundraiser who is great with people but not so proficient at generating those vital follow-up reports. Instead of spending long hours struggling over your desktop, find ways to free up your time for face-to-face contact. To meet your deadlines, get smart about delegating, outsourcing, using new technology, or renegotiating the deskwork that will never be your strong suit.

→ **Choose your companions.** Make choices about how much time to spend with the various people in your life. At work, don't obsess about annoying or unproductive colleagues. As much as possible, disengage yourself from the time-wasters and naysayers. Instead, direct more of your attention to people who may become productive allies.

→ **Look at the data.** Sometimes it is worth examining the actual numbers to determine precisely how much of your time and resources result in most of your achievements. As we discussed in Chapter 21 on managing priorities, a good way to get a more realistic picture of your work patterns is to keep a log for a while. You may be surprised by how few of your activities deliver most of your success.

→ **Simplify.** Applying the Rule is sometimes simply a matter of getting rid of clutter and distractions. If everything seems too complicated, look for ways to get rid of some of the massive 80 percent, so that the vital 20 percent will become more evident. This might require delegating tasks, declining invitations, getting rid of low-value products, simplifying your routines, and reducing the archive of documents and stacks of stuff that you've been saving, just in case.

→ **Pursue your passions.** Identify which 20 percent of your life yields your greatest satisfaction, enjoyment, and sense of well-being, and reflect that knowledge in the way you schedule your time. If being in nature helps to keep you feeling balanced and there's no time on your calendar for a walk in the park, it's time to make a shift.

27

How to Create Mentoring that Works Both Ways

Back in the 1970s, feminists seized on mentoring as a way to help women ease their way through the men's club atmosphere then dominating so many American offices. Through the years, the idea has become mainstream and now there's a widespread understanding that having supportive mentors helps both women and men to advance professionally. But the definition of "mentor" varies widely, and not all career-focused mentoring programs succeed.

What makes structured programs and individual efforts so difficult to get right is that mentoring involves building a relationship between two people. And strong human relationships require a delicate mix of hard work, honest communication, and good luck.

As with any healthy relationship, a mentoring partnership prospers only when both parties receive value. Initially, the mentor may be motivated simply by a desire to give back and to be a good citizen. And early in a relationship the mentee usually does get the most benefit, including sympathetic advice and, sometimes, an active champion at critical moments. But when the relationship really clicks, the mentor eventually receives at least as much as she gives.

If you're the mentor, one of the first rewards is the pleasure of having someone listen to you and the good feeling that flows from him or her following your advice. Then, as a relationship grows, the mentee's questions and feedback can give you a chance to pause and gain a new perspective. Through the long term, your conversations tend to become truly two-way, with both of you seeking advice, sharing insights, and exploring delicate career questions in an environment of trust.

Several of my dearest friendships began decades ago when I agreed to serve as a mentor, motivated simply by a desire to support deserving young professionals. I can't think about mentoring without feeling a wave of gratitude for two particular mentees, Andrea Wilkinson and Sherry Little. When I met these two best friends they were young congressional staffers, thrilled to be working on Capitol Hill, but not always sure about how to build careers in the government.

First Andrea, and later Sherry, asked me to serve as a mentor. Both were obviously talented and I enjoyed their company, so I said "yes" without giving it much thought. At the beginning, we spent much of our time together talking about their work challenges. But soon I was hearing as much good advice as I could offer. Through the years, Andrea and Sherry have pushed me beyond my career comfort zone, sent along clients and opportunities, challenged me to be less self-deprecating, and have been there for all my biggest events.

These strategies can help you create powerful mentoring relationships

Being involved in mentoring can be enormously rewarding, whether you're the guide or the protégée. *If you want to attract additional mentors, or strengthen the relationships you already have, try these tactics:*

→ **To identify mentors, begin with casual connections.** If you hope to recruit a mentor, don't start with complete strangers. Most of these people are too busy and unlikely to make time for you. Instead, look to your network. As we discussed in Chapter 10, your network extends from your inner circle all the way out to communities of folks you haven't even met yet, like members of your professional groups or your college alumni association. Think about the people with whom you have even a slight connection and gradually strengthen some of those relationships, slowly and steadily, one Sugar Grain at a time.

→ **To recruit mentors, request a bit of advice.** All too often, young professionals ask higher-ranking colleagues to serve as mentors, are told "yes," but then nothing happens. Usually it's more effective to gradually engage advisors, starting with a small request and encouraging further involvement as they get to know you better. For example, you might approach a senior colleague and say something like, "I want to get better at X, and I notice that you are great at X, so I wonder if you could give me advice about this X-type challenge?"

→ **For more help, make a specific request.** Some mentors would like to do more, but they don't know where to start. They can't read your mind, and it's often up to you to explain when you need more than advice. So make an explicit request when you want something from a mentor. If programs, procedures, or deadlines are involved, do all the homework, so you make it as easy as possible for them to put in a good word or fight your battles. And understand that it isn't fair to ask for action if your mentor doesn't have suitable rank, access, or knowledge.

→ **Welcome honesty.** At times a mentor's most important contribution is to give constructive feedback, even when it's unpleasant for you to hear it. If you're working on a project in which your mentor has expertise, ask for suggestions about how to improve your chances for success. Don't allow yourself to be offended by honest feedback, even if it is hard to swallow, and resist the urge to respond defensively.

→ **Aim for two-way relationships.** Mentoring works best when both parties make an effort and enjoy some benefit. If you are trying to forge a stronger bond with your mentor, ask yourself what's in it for them. Can you, the mentee, make the relationship more valuable by serving as a source of information and support? Do you know what they care about most? Have you figured out the kinds of activities and venues they prefer?

→ **Practice sponsoring and mentoring.** To learn how to create better relationships, look for opportunities to practice *being* the mentor. Even if you are at the bottom of your hierarchy at work, you can find mentees through alumni and nonprofit networks. As you find ways to make contributions to your mentees, you will get a better sense of how to manage upward and energize your own mentors.

Although there are many reasons to be a mentor, much of the joy comes from helping someone else. If others guided you along your professional path, now is a good time to pay it forward. If you didn't have the help you needed, break the negative cycle by giving someone else the kind of support that would have made your life easier. ***If you want to be a great mentor, consider these suggestions:***

→ **Listen.** You can't solve everything. But you can always help by asking questions in a positive way and genuinely listening to the answers.

→ **Request plans.** When mentees identify realistic goals, suggest that it's time to create a plan. Help them identify action steps and milestones, and hold them accountable for moving forward.

→ **Make connections.** Be alert to opportunities to tap into your own network on behalf of mentees who need information or introductions. Once you build up a bank of mentoring relationships, it can be particularly gratifying when your long-term protégées agree to help out your newest crop of mentees.

→ **Meet regularly.** Don't let strong mentoring relationships fade away after the initial challenges have been addressed. If the match between the two of you still feels right, suggest ways to continue the conversation, even if there is no pressing need. You've both made an investment, and the best part of your partnership may be just beginning.

Reciprocal mentoring can be powerful

The classical image of mentoring involves a relationship where an older, capable person helps to guide someone with less experience and knowledge. That idea of a wise, generous senior advisor leading us along a career path can be wonderful and soothing, but it's not always available or even desirable.

Here's what can make mentoring really hum: creating relationships intended to work both ways.

I thought about this new style of mentoring during a long weekend at our Virginia farmhouse, as I dropped in and out of a three-day conversation between my husband, Andy Alexander, and one of his much younger professional pals. Andy was the longtime Washington bureau chief for the Cox Newspapers chain, where he also ran the international news operation. He won journalism awards and served a term as ombudsman of *The Washington Post*. Once a classic newspaper guy, these days his work includes teaching and fostering media innovation, mainly at Ohio University's Scripps College of Communication.

Andy's 20-something friend Ryan Lytle has racked up an impressive resume as a multimedia expert. An outstanding 2010 Scripps College graduate, today Ryan is a rising star at Mashable.com, a global source of news "for the digital generation."

As the two men brainstormed about trends in delivering the news, what fascinated me about their interaction was the way each one listened so intently and seemed to be learning from the other. When I asked about it, Ryan said one thing he learns from veterans who grew up in a very different news business is how to build organizations and grow leadership. Andy said, "Everything I do professionally is about the future of journalism. And part of being engaged is staying in touch with the people, like Ryan, who are creating that future."

Andy and Ryan didn't create a formal mentoring relationship. But their style of dialogue illustrates the benefits of an emerging concept: *reciprocal* mentoring, where each partner is both teacher and student. Both men enjoy and benefit from their talks. The differences in their age, skill set, and experience are what make their sharing so interesting and valuable. ***If you're ready to give reciprocal mentoring a try, consider this approach:***

→ **Think about the potential exchange.** As a starting point, define what you want to learn and some of the strengths you have to offer. If you have potential partners in mind, approach them with the idea of mutual mentoring. If the problem is that you don't know where to start, spread the word about what you're seeking. Professional, community, and alumni circles can provide venues for meeting people of different generations and backgrounds.

→ **Identify needs and goals.** It's not enough for partners to begin with a vague sense that they'd like some career help. Each partner should enter the process with clear ideas about issues to explore and forms of assistance that would be welcome. Later, when the relationship is successfully launched, it might grow in surprising directions.

→ **Consider logistics.** It's great if you find a mentor in your neighborhood and can meet over coffee or lunch. But what if you go through your national group and find an ideal partner who lives across the country? Explore options like phone calls or video chats, and set a schedule that's comfortable and convenient for both of you.

28

Don't Be Sabotaged by Your Own Frustration

Years ago I learned something about career resilience by watching how two women in the same large organization handled their work-related frustration. Mary* had an abusive boss who bullied her and made her days miserable. She was from a humble background and not as highly educated as some of her colleagues, and she felt shy about confiding in coworkers when the boss insulted and demeaned her. Senior management finally became aware of the boss's ugly habits when he was investigated and fired for unrelated wrongdoing.

Mary knew that she had strong grounds for complaint, but she decided to let go of her hurt and anger and become strategic. In spite of her bad experience, she wanted to stay with the organization, and she convinced management to provide her with training and opportunities in a different professional field. Mary became an excellent student and her confidence grew. As the years went by, she was promoted and ultimately she built a new career that brought her great pride.

Elsewhere in the organization, Cheri* was passed over for several management slots. She was smart, polished, and technically proficient, but was told that she wasn't a good fit for the leadership track she hoped to pursue. Cheri felt entitled to a promotion and was angry about not moving up in the way she'd expected. Instead of listening to the feedback and trying another approach, she fumed and grumbled to anyone who would listen. As Cheri allowed her resentment to grow, her coworkers tired of the chip on her shoulder.

Nobody was sad to see Cheri go when she was hired away by a start-up company. And she didn't resist the urge to fully express her bitterness. In her last week on the job, Cheri told her bosses just what she thought of them. When the start-up quickly failed, nobody on her old team wanted to write her a favorable recommendation. Cheri ultimately had to take a lower-level job in a different field.

Move out of your own way and let go of workplace frustration

Do you arrive home from work too anxious to relax and enjoy your evening? Do you find yourself waking up in the middle of the night, fuming about what they're doing at the office? Do you hear yourself complaining to colleagues about how things are done around here?

Professional life has always been full of annoying jolts and tedious challenges. Some career paths have become increasingly bumpy in recent years, with belt-tightening and increasing demands for production. It's understandable if you're feeling discouraged and indignant about how you've been treated.

But just because there are strong reasons for your negative emotions doesn't mean you can afford to indulge in them. You are in charge of your career. If you hope to stay where you are, and you want things to improve, you need to come up with a plan.

And before you can implement your plan, you may need an attitude adjustment. *Here are reasons to stop fuming and let go of your preoccupation with the bad stuff at work:*

→ **You must be present.** If you want to move to a better career phase, you have to operate in high gear. But if you're preoccupied with how you were treated last week or last year, you can't be fully engaged in what's happening today. If you give in to annoyance, you could be less alert to new opportunities, less creative, and more likely to make mistakes.

→ **You must be energetic.** When you're trying to launch a new plan, it helps to be in great shape. But if you can't let go of your angst, you won't sleep as well, your stress level will slow you down, your health might suffer, and you won't be able to do your best work.

→ **It's best to come across as an upbeat team player.** Your best friends may be willing to listen to the story of your bad breaks, but even they will grow tired of you if you don't move on. Most folks prefer working with positive people, and they tend to avoid the high maintenance whiners. When you find a way to release your negativity, you'll be more productive, work better with others, and attract more opportunities.

Do you feel more like Cheri than Mary? Is it possible that your continuing frustration is undercutting your good work and limiting your career mobility? *If it's time to lose your negative attitude, these strategies can help:*

→ **Notice.** Becoming aware of your frustration can be the first step in letting it go. Take a careful look at how you've been feeling and be honest with yourself about the consequences. Consider keeping a journal of your feelings. Once you have specifically described your misfortune and the pain it caused you, it's much easier to move past it all.

→ **Be grateful.** Neuroscience research suggests that we don't experience gratitude and anxiety at the same time. As a result, your ire will naturally dissipate when you focus on things that cause you to feel thankful. So make a list of things for which you're most grateful and read that list a few times a day, including first thing in the morning and last thing at night.

→ **Take breaks.** By pausing and shifting your focus, you can dispel pent-up antagonism and feel refreshed. Whether it means chatting with a friend, taking a short walk, or spending a few minutes meditating, take frequent breaks throughout the workday. And remember that regular exercise provides a change of pace and can help you feel more cheerful.

→ **Forgive.** When you can't stop being upset about how management has treated you, you're likely to remain bogged down in the past. But when you elect to stop blaming people, you can move beyond yesterday, enjoy today, and look forward to tomorrow. Many spiritual traditions offer guidance about the benefits of and the path to forgiveness.

29

Yes, You Can Do Something about Difficult Colleagues

Does it feel like your job would be more fun if you could work with a different crowd? Are you surrounded by whiners, chronic pessimists, backstabbers, or other difficult people? Or is going to the office less pleasant because of that one person whom you just can't stand?

In any workplace there may be folks who are hard to get along with. Sometimes you can reduce the pain by staying out of their way. But avoiding their company may not be an option. *Here are five suggestions for dealing with your difficult colleague:*

1) **Don't escalate the problem.** The first rule is to not make things worse by indulging in petty revenge, sulking, or gossip about what a jerk that guy is. Even if he started it, the wise move is to take the high road. If you spend too much time complaining behind his back, your colleagues may think that you're just as

bad as he is. When you disagree with him about a project, limit your comments to the work itself. And never get personal.

2) **Confide in a trusted friend or colleague.** Though you don't want to indulge in public rants, it can be helpful to describe the situation to another person. If you're feeling angry, hurt, or frustrated, it's hard to objectively assess your options. Brainstorming with someone may help you identify ways to address the problem and move on.

3) **Understand other personality types.** Just as some are born left-handed and others are right-handed, people tend to fall into various broad personality categories. For example, some of us are extroverts, and we like to brainstorm out loud, sharing our thoughts long before we've reached our conclusions. This can be annoying to introverts who may prefer a quieter environment where people don't start to talk until they know what they want to say. As you learn more about basic personality types, it's easier to recognize when other people's behavior is not about you—it is just how they are made. Tools such as the readily available Myers-Briggs Type Indicator can help you to understand what makes you tick, and suggest strategies for communicating with people whose approach to work is different than yours.

4) **Listen to them in a new way.** Once we start thinking of people as "difficult," we tend to stop hearing what they say. As they speak, we feel defensive, and we start working on our rebuttals instead of paying attention to their points. Most humans aren't skillful at hiding what we feel, so at some level they know we're ignoring them, causing their obnoxious behavior to intensify. You can often defuse a tense situation by putting aside your distrustful response and concentrating on what is being said. By listening closely, you may forge a connection and launch a new era of healthy communications.

5) **Manage your attitude.** Although you can't control other people, you can shift the dynamic by changing how you respond to them. Because you can't really hide your feelings, if you approach someone in a mood of anger, annoyance, or contempt, he'll have some sense of it. And his answer to your negative attitude might

be an even stronger display of fury or rudeness. You can break the negative cycle by adjusting your own emotional state. If you learn to shift the way you feel, you can dramatically change relationships that traditionally have been rocky. ***Try this approach to adjusting your reaction to a colleague:***

- Start by quietly recalling the emotions you experienced the last time you clashed with your difficult colleague. Did you feel hurt, tense, or frustrated? Where in your body did you experience the feelings and tension? Was it in your shoulders or your stomach?

- Now take a few deep breaths. As you breathe, relax your shoulders, clenched fists, or other body parts that feel tight. Visualize each breath as a flow of calm energy, helping to release that tension.

- Now that you're more relaxed, try to imagine an alternative emotional state that might feel better and make it easier for you to deal with the colleague. For example, might it help if you could look at that guy with some sense of compassion?

- Come up with a simple phrase to describe that alternative emotional state such as, "I am calm and have compassion in my heart." Through the next few days, practice repeating the phrase. As you do so, experiment with using it to help yourself feel more relaxed and upbeat.

- Once you've practiced in safe places to summon up your more positive emotional state, try out the technique in more challenging situations. You might use the technique when you're annoyed with a waiter, or placed on hold by a call center. When you feel like you have the knack, call up your positive attitude when you're actually with your difficult colleague. Now that you're able to put aside your bad feelings, they won't have so much power over you. And you might find that their attitude changes, as well.

As we discussed in the last chapter, you won't be able to change many of the frustrating situations in your career. But it's easier to move forward once you've learned how to put your frustration aside.

30

Find or Build Communities

When pundits describe the characteristics of successful entrepreneurs, they may emphasize independent thinking, a tolerance for risk, or the willingness to break rules. But when I try to predict the success of either business owners creating their own thing, or intrapreneurs making their way within large organizations, I tend to look at something else. I find that, though their personalities vary widely, most effective entrepreneurial thinkers seem to share one trait: They understand the power of their networks.

In Chapter 10 we talked about how you might visualize your network as a series of four concentric circles, starting with your core group in Circle #1 and moving out to your far-flung communities in Circle #4. Not everyone actively manages that fourth Circle, but in building your career like an entrepreneur, it's smart to explore the power of your communities.

A "community" is a group that has members, rather than a collection of unconnected people. Membership may be informal or unacknowledged, but the community members are linked by common values or interests. And often they have some feeling of belonging, as well as a sense of mattering—of being able to make a difference to the group.

Among your communities are your neighbors, people with a history or interest similar to yours, professionals who share your training and challenges, and members of the clubs and associations you have formally joined.

Your communities are packed with people you may never have met. But when you approach someone as a member of your group, it's unlikely he'll treat you like a stranger. Your communities are a source of business intelligence, customers, mentors, referrals, and friends.

There's a growing body of research that links good health with one's degree of social connection. That reflects not just relationships within your inner circle, but also your interaction with broader communities. Reasons for the health impact might be that supportive communities can help you to manage stress, gain perspective, and maintain healthy habits.

Beyond that, your emotions and behaviors can be influenced by the emotions and behaviors of those in your extended communities. Research on human networks suggests that your attitude and habits may be shaped or reinforced not only by your close contacts, but also by your contacts' contacts, and their contacts as well. If the people in your communities are energetic, helpful, and creative, their positive vibes can be contagious, helping you to stay positive as you push your boundaries.

No matter how busy they might otherwise be, successful entrepreneurs are often highly attuned to their business, customer, and social communities, looking to them for inspiration, technical knowledge, clients, and empathy. Molly Peterson, the photographer who shot the photo on the back of this book, is a fine example of a modern entrepreneur who is investing in her communities as she continues to invent her multifaceted career.

Molly's documentary-style photos are beautiful and authentic and have been widely published. She is known particularly for her food and farm shots, and she took the pictures for *Growing Tomorrow*, a 2015 book with portraits of 18 sustainable farmers. Photography is only one of Molly's professions. She and her husband run Heritage Hollow Farms, where they raise grass-fed livestock and also operate a farm store in Sperryville, Virginia.

Although it seems that two active careers would take up all Molly's time, she's one of those natural givers and connectors, active in both community and online groups. I bump into her at meetings of a nonprofit board and also via social media, where she has built a broad following. It was through customer and online communities that Molly came up with one of the farms' distribution channels. She noticed that many Washington, D.C., residents care about the benefits of sustainable meat but can't always make the two-hour drive to

Sperryville or be available for a scheduled delivery. So she arranged for meat orders to be delivered to freezers installed in Washington area Crossfit Gyms.

When I asked Molly why she's so active in the community, despite her heavy schedule, she said, "I was taught from a young age by both of my parents to be curious, connected, and 'well rounded.' They were both entrepreneurs, as were many of my extended family members. I've always been curious and interested in a world outside of my own: Why do people do what they do, is there a deeper reason for it, what makes them 'tick'? I also feel it never hurts to ask; nothing frustrates me more than when I'm told that something can't be done simply because that isn't the way it's usually done."

Molly also said, "Outside of my careers I have a genuine care and concern for my community and the Earth and how to make it better, more joy-filled, healthier—whether that's through my photography as art, through the way we raise our livestock that ultimately feeds families, or through my time. It's a fine balancing act to strive to keep all the pieces in line, but my brain rarely slows down. I carry a notebook with me everywhere to make sure I keep on track with all of the daily tasks and requests."

Become active in your existing communities, or discover new ones

Staying in touch with a range of supportive communities can be key to building your resilient career. *These strategies can help you to develop deeper community involvement:*

→ **Identify your communities.** Start by listing groups of people with whom you are already associated. This might include groups related to places where you worked or went to school, professional associations, neighborhood committees, and online groups. Then think about topics or activities that interest you, and search for additional organizations of like-minded people. If you're an Italian American who likes to raise herbs and cook, look around for a garden club, gourmet group, or Italian-American association.

→ **Become active.** Study the list of the organizations you belong to now, as well as those you might like to join. Target a few communities where you'd like to raise your profile and build relationships. Then look for opportunities to make a contribution. This might mean volunteering for a service project, joining a committee, or simply attending functions.

→ **Care about an issue.** Many communities are built around causes or local needs. If your family has been touched by cancer, you may want to join a committee that raises money for research. If you're concerned about children in your town who live in poverty, join the local pantry organization or a big sisters group. The best way to get to know people can be working with them to address a problem you all care about.

→ **Be a mentor.** To connect with a younger crowd or make your network more diverse, offer to serve as a mentor. Contact a professional association, or get in touch directly with someone who is starting something new, and volunteer to share your skill set or be an advisor.

→ **Give money.** If you're overwhelmingly busy right now, you can quietly begin to build name recognition by making contributions to nonprofit groups. If your name shows up repeatedly on donor lists, group leaders may eventually beg you to become more actively involved.

→ **Launch a new group.** If you're passionate about an activity or cause, don't be discouraged if you can't find an organization for people who feel the same way. It can be surprisingly easy to start your own group. Use social media, community bulletin boards, newspaper ads, or other mechanisms to publicize your interest. Your first event might be anything from a Twitter chat to a coffee date with one other person. Other people love communities, and they might be willing to join yours, particularly if you're willing to do a lot of the work.

31

Make Your Meeting Time More Productive

How much time do you devote to meetings? You might want to say, "Too much!" But seriously, do you have any idea what percentage of your work life is spent meeting with people? Try calculating it. If meetings take just 20 percent of your time, and you work 40 hours a week, 50 weeks a year, that's a whopping 400 hours annually.

Just think about what you'd be able to accomplish if you could retrieve only 10 percent of that meeting time. You would have a whole week to devote to your top priorities.

In fact, if you start to rethink your approach to meetings, you can find ways both to spend less time at conference tables, and also to get more value from the meetings that you do attend. *Start by trying out these strategies to reduce the hours you spend in meetings:*

→ **Cut them short.** Explore with your colleagues whether some regular meetings could be shortened. For example, if your team always gathers on Monday mornings for 90 minutes, aim for a new time limit of one hour. And if other meetings typically last one or one-half hour, could you all agree to cut them down to 45 or 20 minutes? An extra bonus of shortened meetings will be the gap between your standard ending and starting times. Participants in your 10 o'clock will be late less often because they'll now have a chance to take a break or check their e-mail after their nine o'clock ends at 9:45 a.m.

→ **Stand up or walk around.** Another way to encourage shorter meetings is to occasionally schedule quick standing meetings, where nobody takes the time to sit down. And an approach that works well for some kinds of topics is the walking meeting, where two or three of you will stroll for half an hour, as you talk through your issues. This can happen inside, in large or connected buildings, or outside, perhaps in nearby parks. I know a leader who twice a week has a 30-minute walk-and-talk time block on her calendar. Any staff member can sign up to be her walking companion, and if the slot is left open, she may invite a staffer she rarely has a chance to see.

→ **Say no.** You might also reduce your time in meetings by getting better at declining invitations. Of course, many meetings are useful or required. But sometimes your participation isn't all that important, and you can be excused simply by explaining that you have another commitment (which might mean your scheduled time at your desk).

→ **Create a no-meeting day.** Finally, consider working out an agreement with your team members for a meeting-free time zone. If you all decide to keep Wednesday free of meetings, you can plan on one day a week for telecommuting or concentrating on your top priority projects.

When you run the meetings, keep them productive with these strategies

Some of your most valuable meetings are the ones where you're in charge. And if you're the leader, you have an opportunity to make better use of your time and theirs by tweaking the routine. *Here are nine basic rules for running effective meetings:*

1) **Know the purpose.** Before you send out invitations, be clear about your goals in calling a meeting. When no business is pressing, or work can be accomplished more easily in another way, be flexible about cancelling regular meetings. Leaders known for holding pointless meetings may have a tough time attracting participation when they really need it.

2) **Have an effective invitation process.** For successful meetings, you might have to be assertive about sending invitations and reminding participants of the details.

   ◆ Even if it's a regular meeting and everybody knows the drill, specify the date, day, time, and place.

   ◆ Routinely send at least one reminder, at the last minute.

   ◆ If you're using e-mail for invitations or reminders, put the details in the subject line.

   ◆ If it might be useful, share the proposed attendance list.

3) **Create an agenda.** A written list of discussion items helps to shape participants' expectations and keep the meeting on target. This is true even when the gathering consists of just two or three team members talking through their issues over coffee. It often makes sense to ask attendees for discussion items and to distribute the agenda in advance.

4) **Build in structure.** Even informal meetings should feel intentional. As the leader or convener, plan to include in each meeting:

   ◆ **An opening** in which you state the purpose and the desired outcome.

   ◆ **A middle** in which agenda items are discussed, with each one being moved forward by at least a baby step.

   ◆ **A closing** when you may sum up the conclusions, action items, and assignments, and perhaps mention next steps or future events. It is also appropriate to thank people for their attendance and contributions.

5) **Warm it up.** There's a legitimate social component to many meetings, and you may make more progress if all the participants feel engaged and comfortable about offering comments. You can

address some social needs and establish a cordial mood for the event by devoting the first five or 10 minutes to a warm-up phase in which everyone is invited to offer information, suggestions, or concerns. This can be as simple as brief introductions, or you might request brief answers to a question such as: "Do you have any good news to report?"

6) **Set the tone.** Treat all participants with courtesy, give speakers your full attention, and don't work on other projects during the meeting. If you have trouble staying focused, try taking notes of the discussion. Show your respect for attendees by making sure your meetings always start and end on schedule.

7) **Establish ground rules.** Regular meetings will flow more smoothly if everybody understands the etiquette. Set the rules or build a consensus on matters such as:

   ◆ Attendance.

   ◆ Arrival times.

   ◆ Participation in discussions.

   ◆ Use of cell phones and other devices.

   ◆ Confidentiality.

8) **Keep track.** Every meeting should have someone designated to keep a record, at least of key conclusions and assignments. This can be as simple as your rough notes—the ones that you, the leader, use when you summarize the meeting in your closing remarks.

9) **Follow up.** After the meeting, be sure that both the participants and the invitees who couldn't attend are sent a copy of the notes. Consider touching base with participants who left with assignments, checking that they have everything they need, and are moving forward on their tasks. If nothing seems to come of your meetings, people will lose interest and stop taking them seriously.

Get more from the meetings you don't run

No matter how well you manage the meetings you run, and how successful you are at avoiding some others, you probably still spend a big chunk of your work time convening with colleagues. So your next challenge is to make that remaining meeting time as productive as possible.

That was a valuable lesson for my client Sharon*, who didn't understand why she hadn't been given the chance to lead a team. Sharon groused to her mentor, "If I didn't have to waste so much time sitting in their useless meetings, I could really show them what I can do."

The mentor countered, "You can't get out of those meetings, so why not make better use of them? That's where people see you in action, so think of those sessions as a chance to show off your strengths. Instead of coming in late and acting distracted, aim to look like one of the most productive people there."

Convinced it was worth a try, *Sharon developed a five-point plan for being a stellar attendee at each required meeting:*

1) **Prep.** She'd rearrange her priorities to allow a little time for preparation, like reading the agenda and the background materials sent out in advance.

2) **Plan remarks.** While prepping, she'd identify at least two comments or questions to contribute to the discussion.

3) **Focus on the purpose.** She'd ask herself, "What's the goal of this meeting? And what can I do to help get us there?"

4) **Create goals.** Before arriving, she'd set a personal objective like, "Today I'll come across as calm and organized."

5) **Focus through writing.** Once the discussion began, she'd listen carefully to each speaker, taking notes to help her stay focused.

Sharon's plan worked. Meeting leaders began noticing that she seemed more engaged and was adding to the discussion. They started to count on her active participation, and that led to her getting better project assignments. After six months, she was appointed team leader for an exciting project.

To her surprise, once Sharon launched her five-point plan, she found it brought other benefits beyond just looking like a more effective meeting participant. Once she developed the habit of always being prepared, her job started to feel more interesting and satisfying. Also, she became aware that the growing respect for her as a participant continued after each meeting. Soon she felt more connected to her colleagues. And she had fewer moments of boredom and frustration. "By trying to *act* engaged," she said, "I found out that it's more fun to *be* engaged."

The fact is that meetings represent a big part of your life as a professional. And as long as you have to spend the time, why not get more back from it? *Here are six strategies for maximizing the return on the hours you spend in other people's meetings:*

1) **Do the homework.** You won't fool anybody when you're searching through your papers or tablet, trying to catch up with the crowd. When you put the meeting time on the calendar, schedule some time for any necessary preparation.

2) **Be prompt.** Even if the culture tolerates casual start times, late arrivers show a lack of respect for their more punctual colleagues. By typically being there at the appointed hour, you can help to set a more productive tone. And once you're there, you can make use of any delay by reviewing the materials or networking with the crew.

3) **Understand the intention.** It's easy to dismiss many meetings as pointless, but that doesn't get you anywhere. Somebody had something in mind or you wouldn't be sitting in that room. You'll be able to make a bigger contribution if you have some sense of the objective. Dig a little, and you may find several reasons why you've all been called in, such as:

   ◆ Sharing information.

   ◆ Brainstorming and solving specific problems.

   ◆ Establishing goals, making plans, and keeping track of milestones.

   ◆ Creating a collective sense of purpose.

   ◆ Encouraging collaboration by helping people get to know each other.

4) **Set your own goals.** Of course, you always want to do your part to make the meeting productive. But beyond that, you'll get more out of your participation if you have your own games to play. For example, if you're trying to broaden your brand, your objective might be to speak knowledgeably about areas outside your normal portfolio.

5) **Listen.** One reason so many sessions feel useless is that attendees just aren't paying attention. If just one or two of you start really

listening, you can change the tone. And if you make a habit of being truly engaged, chances are that when it's your turn somebody will hear what you have to say.

6) **Follow up.** Often, the success of a meeting depends on what happens next. Do your bit. Keep track of any commitments you make and do that work. If you're particularly interested in aspects of the conversation, find ways to continue the dialogue later. And let people know if you found their remarks to be helpful.

If meetings are part of the job, complaining about them is simply a waste of time. Instead, strategize to get as much as you can from the hours spent around a conference table.

32

How to Love Your Work Again

Author Kerry Hannon, who wrote the foreword to this book, is a noted authority on work and career. For the last two decades, she has been covering all aspects of business and personal finance as an author, columnist, editor, and writer for leading media organizations including the *New York Times*, *Forbes*, *Money*, *PBS*, *U.S. News & World Report*, and the *Wall Street Journal*. Although I've learned much from Kerry's careful research, what has inspired me the most is her own career path.

Kerry started as a traditional print journalist, earning a salary from major publications. Then about 14 years ago she struck out on her own, freelancing for some of the nation's top magazines and newspapers. But she does so much more. Kerry has become a prolific author, a peripatetic speaker, a frequent radio and TV guest, and an expert panelist at conferences. This entrepreneurial dynamo has become a one-woman media company. And all along the way she has helped other writers, given generously of her time to nonprofits, pursued her love of horses, traveled with her husband, and stayed in touch with her friends.

In recent years, Kerry has published countless articles and several books about how to follow your heart in order to find the work you love. Pursuing the topic of "second acts," she has traveled back and forth across the country, interviewing folks who have reinvented their work lives, and speaking frequently about how to navigate midcareer transitions.

Kerry says that many people dream of starting over with an entirely different kind of career. But what she's been hearing is that, all too often, that kind of big shift may not be practical. So, in a 2015 book, Kerry changed gears to focus on how to make your *current* job more satisfying. I had the pleasure of serving as an expert for the book and loved the chance to brainstorm with Kerry, learning from her many stories, and talking about the rapidly changing American workplace.

Kerry Hannon says you can find more fun and meaning at your current job

Love Your Job: The New Rules for Career Happiness is Kerry's guide for people who are looking to find or reignite purpose and joy in their work. She says, "If you want to be happier, you have to do something, to take action." That doesn't always mean a big swerve from the past. "It does, however, often call on the courage to make necessary but sometimes uncomfortable and even painful changes." ***If you are ready to take action, here are seven tips from Kerry's book:***

1) **Begin with a journal.** Kerry suggests you dedicate a notebook or computer file to your "Job Remodeling Journal." Launch your effort by writing for 20 minutes every day for a week. Let yourself go as you talk about what you'd love to see in your dream job. Perhaps you can list people who seem happy at work so you can ask them about what they enjoy in their career. Next, try writing about the times your professional life was most rewarding. Kerry recommends that you create a "budget" in which you list the pros and cons at work. From there, start planning action steps for building on the best parts of your job and addressing the liabilities.

2) **Know when it's burnout.** Sometimes you're feeling miserable, but the problem is not really that you hate your job. As you journal, you may realize that the biggest issue is you're just too tired.

Job burnout can be experienced as physical, emotional, or mental exhaustion combined with self-doubt and uncertainty about the value of your work. If you're feeling burnt out, the solution must start with you and goes beyond what happens at the office. Consider taking a vacation, or perhaps a series of shorter breaks. And look closely at your health and fitness programs.

3) **Stop complaining.** According to Kerry, "It's remarkably easy to fall into the trap of whining and grumbling about a boss, coworker, or employer, but it rarely makes things better." Her advice is blunt: "Do something. Get over it." Sometimes you can't make progress until you "stop the looping chatter." Kerry suggests that you read over your journal, looking for the specific things you can change. Start working on those aspects of your job by identifying small steps.

4) **Get in shape financially.** Human resources professionals say that personal financial challenges are a frequent cause of employee stress, poor health, and low productivity. If money problems keep you up at night, your work suffers. On the other hand, Kerry says, being financially fit gives you the freedom to make choices because "you are not trapped and held ransom by your paycheck." Kerry urges you to do everything possible to eliminate debt. The relief can transform your work life.

5) **Enrich your job.** Kerry says that making a number of small tweaks to your current job can help it become more interesting and full of opportunity. As a start, stay informed about the trends in your field. "Just being in the know can inspire you to think of projects and tasks." Also, find ways to do even more of the kind of work you like best. And, at the same time, search for additional kinds of duties. When your bosses ask you to take on another task, "accept the invitation gratefully . . . and then figure out how to do it," she says. Another strategy for job enhancement is to network more actively with colleagues. Reach out to people you don't know well, look your coworkers in the eye, find opportunities to smile and chat—and keep building new connections.

6) **Create more flexibility.** "When I ask people to name one thing that would make them happier about their jobs, they say independence in some way, shape, or form," Kerry says. The option to

work flexibly gives us a sense of autonomy, and that is a good way to make your work life immensely more enjoyable. Two increasingly popular ways to give you back some control are telecommuting and flexible work schedules. "When you feel trapped and micromanaged in your office environment, the sense of control of your own time and virtual freedom can do wonders to help you get reconnected with your work again," she says.

7) **Learn new tricks.** "If you're feeling stuck in your job and don't know what to do next, charge up your brain cells," Kerry says. Even if you have only a hazy notion of what interests you, start exploring libraries, classes, or the Web, and learn something new.

The core message from Kerry's book, in her words, is that "*you* can turn it around and rebound from your malaise or grim work environment. *You* have to own it. *You* consciously choose whether to continue being unhappy or pick an alternate path and change it up, even if it's in baby steps."

33

Make Social Media Work for You

My normally cheerful client Brian* was aggravated. He'd been assigned to find productive work for Jason*, a new hire. The problem, he said, is that "we can't give Jason a project because he doesn't know how to do anything at all."

Jason had polished manners, an Ivy League education, and a distant family connection to the CEO. Brian's boss had recruited Jason from his last job, where he'd maintained a fairly high profile as a "senior policy advisor."

"Does he really not understand those policy issues?" I asked.

"Oh, he knows the issues alright," Brian said. "But that's irrelevant because he can't *do* anything. We're going to have to find a way to let him go."

It turned out that Jason had enjoyed one of the last remaining old-school jobs, where he wrote all his papers on a legal pad. "He doesn't even know how to use e-mail," Brian said. "In this company, not even the CEO writes longhand drafts for some secretary to type up. I don't care how smart or connected he is. There's no room here for a guy without basic skills."

The fact is that there's no room in most corporations for a professional without basic communication skills. But the definition of those skills can vary widely. During the interview process, nobody at Brian's company asked Jason whether he could use a laptop because it seemed inconceivable that an expert could operate in the policy arena without the "basic skill" of turning out quick drafts and distributing them electronically to the world.

In regard to communications, "basic skills" may seem to include whatever technologies you happen to be using now, but not much more. Too many professionals seem to share the view of my client who said, "I have all the communication skills I need and I'm not going to go messing around with a time sink like social media."

Consider this statement as a SHOUT: Understanding social media is now a *basic skill* in the world of business, academia, or government. That doesn't mean that you have to know how to *do* everything. But you absolutely must understand the fundamental concept and potential power of these rapidly evolving media. Even if you're in your 20s, you'll sound like a dinosaur if you make derisive comments like, "Oh, I just think Twitter is silly. Why would I want to see what some stranger has for lunch?"

Every professional needs a social media strategy

In Chapter 4 we talked about how—whether you know it or not—you have a personal brand that is impacting the opportunities that come along in your career. One factor shaping your brand is the way you show up online. And—whether you know it or not—you do have an online image. If there isn't much information online about you, you may come across as someone not well connected in the world of work.

You are in charge of your career, and it's your responsibility to think about how the Internet and social networking may impact your professional brand. *If you are just starting to think about your social media strategy, consider these four tips:*

1) **Know who's using it.** Most businesses and large organizations now have some kind of social media presence. It's smart to know how your employer, your customers, and your competitors are showing up. If you do nothing else, remain aware of messages flowing from the organizations that matter to your work life.

2) **Set up a profile.** LinkedIn.com, by definition, is a professional networking tool, and many people now use it as a digital address book. It's a great way to gather data and keep track of most of your business associates in one place. But it's become much more than that. Hiring organizations and executive search firms use it on a regular basis to locate talent. And there's a good chance that anyone you meet will use LinkedIn to quickly check you out. So here's a chance to tweak your brand: Create a LinkedIn profile that at least describes your current professional persona.

3) **Get news.** Until you get the hang of it, Twitter feels like a large, random crowd of people shouting about trivia. But once you understand how to organize the flow, it's a tool for connecting with people all over the world in real time. If you want instant feedback from an audience or customer group, Twitter works as well as anything out there. And if you want to know what people are talking about right now, Twitter is your tool.

   Many users never Tweet a word, but they manage Twitter as their primary source of incoming news. Twitter allows you to organize reports from all the major media companies, as well as the specialized journals and commentators you most respect. And it brings fast access to crowdsourced reporting when there's breaking news like an earthquake or security breach. If you'd rather use Facebook or other social options for getting the news, that's fine. But when there's a crisis it helps to be plugged in to some kind of social media stream.

   And if you want to give Twitter a try, please follow me at: @beverlyejones.

4) **Don't mock what you don't understand.** There are so many new channels that it's easy to become bored or confused. Don't think you have to understand it all or feel pressure to sign up for everything from Facebook and Pinterest to Scoop.it and Academia.edu. If you're just starting out, a smart goal is to try one or two tools immediately, and gradually learn more about some of the other options. What you don't want to do is self-righteously refuse to try the tools that your colleagues are using, or make fun of media that you're unwilling to use.

Social media can help you put your best foot forward and stay abreast of developments that are critical to your professional life. If you refuse to even try them, you may find yourself on the wrong side of a great divide. Like today's elderly who don't hear from grandkids because they can't text or e-mail, you might eventually be cut off from your younger or sharper friends and colleagues. The challenge is to understand what is technically possible, and what avenues are your best choice for staying in touch with the people and activities you care about.

10/10/16

34

Stress Is Contagious and Debilitating— but Manageable

You're still tired from working late last night. Your commute this morning was a nightmare and you reached the office 30 minutes behind schedule. Your boss was waiting for you when you arrived, in a hurry to hand over a tedious project with an unreasonable deadline. And you need immediate relief from a coworker who's been grouchy and uncooperative for days.

Feeling stressed out?

You're not alone. Surveys suggest that work is the leading cause of adult stress, and a growing number of workers are experiencing physical or emotional symptoms of job-related stress. Many of my clients not only suffer from stress themselves, but also worry about how a stressful environment might be hurting their teams.

For you, the modern professional, there's bad news and good news. The bad news is that the consequences of chronic stress can be serious, even deadly. The good news is that there are many options for dealing with stress, and you *do* have the power to stop feeling so stressed out.

Understand that stress poses a serious health risk

In some work circles, it seems like the symptoms of stress carry a certain prestige. And occasionally when you complain about feeling stressed, you're actually a bit pleased with yourself and are letting folks know that you've been working hard for the good of the team.

If that rings a bell, please take a careful look at what stress can do to you and get serious about taking control of your health and well-being.

To understand how stress operates, think of it as associated with the "fight-or-flight response," which is our normal reaction to some form of threat or challenge. That response is a kind of survival mechanism that allows humans to automatically react to possible danger. In effect, stress reactions start out as your body's helpful way to generate a bit more oomph when you need it.

Imagine that you're strolling along a country path and you spot a snake up ahead. You freeze for a moment, staring at the snake. While you pause, still uncertain, your brain starts sending messenger chemicals like adrenaline and cortisol that change operations throughout your body. For example, your pulse and blood pressure go up, and more blood flows to your heart and brain. Your body is getting ready to tackle the snake or turn around and run. At the same time, to free up resources, cortisol and other chemicals slow body functions that aren't critical in an emergency, like digestion, your immune system, and your reproductive drive.

This is an example of "acute stress"—a one-time reaction that gives you a burst of energy and helps you fight with or escape from something threatening. Occasional acute stress reactions might even be good for you, strengthening your immune system and helping you to become stronger.

Now let's imagine that, as you stand staring at the snake, you realize that it's actually just a stick lying across the path. Wow, what a relief. You now experience a "relaxation response," which is the opposite of your "fight or flight" reaction. Your chemical balances return to normal, your breathing and heart rates go down again, and you're ready to resume your walk.

On a workday, the stimulant that triggers your stress reaction might be anything from a physical threat to worrisome thoughts. It could come in the form of aggressive drivers cutting you off on the road, your boss giving you that annoying project, or a nasty comment from your obnoxious colleague. But unlike the snake scenario, the moment of stress isn't quickly resolved. Before you can relax, the first stressor is followed by a difficult client call, then a problematic e-mail message, and a plea for help from a panic-stricken colleague.

What you're experiencing now is chronic stress set off by a continuing stream of stimuli. Instead of dropping to normal, your level of hormones like cortisol stays elevated. It's possible to fall into a downward spiral, where stressful events trigger your physical and psychological symptoms, which in turn make your stress level feel even worse. The long-term activation of your stress-response system can disrupt many of your body's processes, threatening your health in many ways.

Chronic stress is associated with numerous health and emotional problems, including:

- → **Physical aches and pains,** such as headaches, back pain, sore necks, and shoulders, and other symptoms such as indigestion.

- → **Sleep difficulties** and feelings of fatigue even when you do sleep.

- → **Cognitive difficulties,** including forgetfulness, constant worry, and an inability to concentrate, be creative, or make decisions.

- → **Emotional symptoms,** including crying, anxiety, anger, loneliness, and a sense of being powerless.

- → **Depression,** which is magnified by stress and can also lead to more stress.

- → **Excess weight,** in part because cortisol can stimulate your appetite and stimulate enzymes to cause fat to be stored in your fat cells.

There are many ways to address stress

There is no single solution to the problem of workplace stress. At times you can address some of the underlying issues. For example, if your long commute is getting you down, perhaps you could arrange to telecommute a day or two a week. But many factors contributing to a stressful environment are beyond your control.

However, even where you can't do much to change your situation, you *can* change your reaction to some of those stressors. You can start feeling better quickly by using one or more of the many techniques shown to be effective in addressing the *symptoms* of stress. Research suggests that just knowing you have a plan in place can be enough to help you calm down and start to mend.

Your doctor and many kinds of therapists and programs might help you come up with a comprehensive plan. Meanwhile, ***here are some of the many practices that can help bring your stress to a more tolerable level:***

→ **Exercise.** Regular walking or other aerobic exercise can significantly reduce the physical symptoms of stress and improve your mood. Repetitive or rhythmic exercises, such as jogging, dancing, or biking, seem to be particularly effective.

→ **Talk to somebody.** The sense of isolation that hits some overworked professionals can magnify the impact of other stressors. Find ways to have meaningful conversations more frequently. Beyond that, make eye contact, actually listen to other people, and try to connect with them in casual ways throughout your day.

→ **Connect with nature.** Research suggests that being in nature—or being aware of nature through something as simple as looking at houseplants—can reduce your stress symptoms. For some people, regular lunchtime walks in a park can make a big difference.

→ **Be creative.** It can be healthy to focus on something different, and stimulate the creative part of your brain. Try painting or playing a musical instrument, working in your garden, taking a cooking class, or taking up a repetitive craft like knitting.

→ **Write about it.** Keeping a journal is a great way to develop insights, change your perspective, and grapple with tension. Try writing about your stressors, describing precisely how they make you feel. Then write about the good parts of your situation, and the things that make you feel grateful. Describe your goals, and the kind of work life you intend to create in the future.

→ **Look at the big picture.** An immediate problem can lose its impact when you place it in perspective. One way to do this is to make a list in your journal about the things that matter most in your life. Then ask yourself: how does the current problem affect your list of big-picture goals or values?

→ **Simplify.** A common source of stress is having too much going on. You may be able to reduce your stress by finding ways to streamline. Look for activities and responsibilities that could be reduced or restructured. And find ways to get rid of physical clutter; getting rid of piles of stuff can feel quite liberating.

→ **Help other people.** In her TED talk, "How to Make Stress Your Friend," health psychologist Kelly McGonigal describes research suggesting that people who reach out to other people reduce their own stress level and build resilience. Your caring for others is associated with a release of the hormone oxytocin, which helps to heal stress induced damage.

→ **Meditate.** In recent years, a wave of studies has explained some of the physiological benefits of meditation. There's evidence that it not only can make you feel more peaceful and physically relaxed, but it also promotes cognitive and psychological changes that enhance your performance and bring a feeling of contentment. In working with clients, I find that it's worth trying a few approaches in order to select a style of meditation that feels comfortable. *Here's a very simple meditation exercise to get you started:*

1) Pick a focus word, short phrase, or prayer that has meaning for you, such as "peace," "Hail Mary, full of grace," or "I am calm and connected."

2) Sit quietly in a comfortable position.

3) Close your eyes.

4) Relax your muscles, progressing from your feet to your calves, thighs, and abdomen, and up to your shoulders, neck, and head.

5) Breathe slowly and naturally, and as you do, say your phrase silently to yourself, each time you inhale and exhale.

6) When thoughts come to mind, just notice them and gently return to your repetition. You might say to yourself, "Oh well," or "That's just a thought."

7) Some instructors suggest that you continue for 10 to 30 minutes, but I find that even a few minutes can be helpful.

Help your team by managing your stress

If you're thinking like a CEO, you want the other members of your team to feel motivated, energetic, and positive. And that requires addressing the level of stress in the environment. If you're the leader and some of the stress is associated with a tough situation, keep your team informed about what's going on and show that you're there to support them. And don't micromanage. It's easier for workers to cope with difficult challenges when they have some control over how to get things done.

What could be most important in difficult circumstances is how you handle yourself. Regardless of whether you're the leader, you can often improve a situation by working hard to stay positive and being willing to listen. Beyond that, the way you manage *your* level of stress can impact the stress level of your colleagues. That's because a stress reaction can be contagious. You can make a difference to colleagues by staying calm and modeling healthy habits, such as taking walking breaks. If your stress level is under control, not only will you be healthier and happier, but also other people will enjoy being around you.

35

Snap Out of It: Coping with Career Rejection

A highly qualified professional went after his dream job. Paul* has an extraordinary record of accomplishment, and he was confident that he'd be the winning candidate. Then he felt devastated when he didn't get the job. Paul wrote me about the intensity of his reaction.

"I hate how this news makes me feel," Paul said. "Not only did I miss out on a job that I really wanted, but the company hired someone against whom I stacked up very well."

"Aside from frustration and sadness, I also have second-order emotions about this decision," Paul said. "Namely, I'm angry at myself for feeling sad and frustrated. These aren't becoming emotions of a gentleman, and certainly I know rationally that they aren't the 'right way' to deal with rejection."

That was almost two years ago, and Paul has long since bounced back. He suggested that his struggles and our e-mail dialogue about career rejection might be useful to others trying to get over a career disappointment. *These tips helped Paul, and they might help you if you don't get that job:*

→ **Know that pain is normal.** As someone who has read a lot of history, Paul realized that all great leaders face setbacks on their paths to glory. But that knowledge didn't help him feel better. He was embarrassed about experiencing such pain from something that happens to everyone.

"I understand your frustration and the other emotions swirling around," I wrote to Paul. "This is a normal passage for all high achievers. Everybody gets rejected eventually, and the pain is tougher when you are not used to it." Knowing it's normal to feel bad was helpful to Paul, and he chose to let go of those secondary emotions, such as guilt for feeling grief.

→ **Write about your pain.** A useful way of dealing with emotional or physical pain is to examine it. When you carefully notice details about your pain, you can develop some distance from it. I suggested that Paul take notes about exactly what he was experiencing. I asked him, "What does it feel like to be 'sad and frustrated'? Can you describe your feelings precisely? Where do you feel tightness or discomfort in your body? What thoughts keep popping into your head? Are you making yourself feel worse by speculating what this disappointment could mean for the future?"

→ **Share with your inner circle.** A key to Paul's rapid recovery is the support he received from his partner and a few close friends. "I found it really helpful just to share my anxieties with them because good friends who know you well can help you maintain perspective," he said.

→ **Understand what you lost.** When you face professional rejection, some of your sadness is a sense of loss because you won't have the opportunity you sought. But sometimes people feel awful about not getting a job they didn't even care about. They like winning and feel bad about losing whether or not they care about the prize. It may help you refocus on the future if you can clearly identity what hurts. Are you mostly concerned about the opportunity, the prestige, or the money? The more you understand the true cause of your disappointment, the better you will be at articulating your next goals and shifting your focus to the future.

→ **Keep a gratitude journal.** As we've discussed, one of the best antidotes for negative emotion is gratitude. When you feel grateful, the part of your brain associated with anxiety quiets down. So you can pull yourself out of a bad place by summoning up a sense of appreciation for the things in your life and career that are going well. A useful exercise is to take a few minutes at the end of every day to list five things for which you're grateful.

→ **Be gracious in defeat.** Though Paul was honest about how he felt with a trusted few, for most of the world he put on his game face, thanked everyone involved in the hiring process, and avoided any show of disappointment. That worked out well for him because one of the executives involved in the hiring decision kept him in mind. Later, she reached out to him and helped him win a job that was an even better fit.

In the depth of his despair, Paul asked, "What's the silver lining here?" One answer is that you can learn how to navigate career transitions, and overcoming setbacks is part of the learning process. And, I said, "Now that you finally have this big disappointment out of the way, you'll start to build up antibodies for the next time, like with chicken pox."

36

How to Foster Great Teams, Even if You're Not the Leader

When I want a quick sense of whether a new client is working well with a team, I take a look at how the members communicate.

Jenna* was an agency branch chief who wanted to help her 14 direct reports become more innovative and productive. Years ago, her branch had been organized into cascading layers, with three deputy chiefs each managing two to four people. That kind of top-down organization made sense when it was the only way to assure the distribution of accurate information. But the old command-and-control model became out of date with the advent of e-mail and other technology. Now that the agency was much flatter, its leaders were exploring new ways to arrange the workload.

To foster collaboration and mentoring, Jenna had organized her group into project-focused teams. Because each person might be on more than one team, and some teams included professionals from other branches, Jenna was keeping her eye on six teams, each with three to five members. Several teams were active, energetic, and highly productive. But a couple of them had gone dormant even before they really got started.

As part of an effort to evaluate and restructure the teams, Jenna asked me to interview each branch employee. Don*, an experienced and technically gifted lawyer, led one of the teams that hadn't gelled. When I asked Don about how his team operated, he said he called meetings "only when they were absolutely necessary." He said he was available to answer individual questions, but he didn't want to encourage people "to waste time talking about each other's problems."

I said to myself, "Wow! Don's poor team never had a chance." Don had no idea that frequent and effective communications are key to building an effective team.

It's long been intuitively obvious that talking is a basic step in teambuilding. But recent research, including studies from the new science of mapping communication patterns, suggests that *how* team members talk with one another may be more important than what they say. Frequent contact is so vital that regular social conversation during breaks could be as crucial as business talk during formal project meetings.

In a flourishing team, communication is constant. Members connect directly with one another, and not just with the leader. Also, the leader circulates actively, visiting with everyone, listening at least as much as talking, and making sure all members get a chance to express their views.

Though communication is key, teams also need structure

Even if you're not the designated leader, you can help shape the culture, support other members, and clarify processes that will help your team to be productive. *These six strategies can help you to strengthen your team:*

1) **Define it.** Be clear about the basics. Members should know who is on the team and who is not, as well as what they're supposed to be doing together.

2) **Model respect and positivity.** Be relentlessly upbeat and treat everyone with respect. In healthy teams, every member's contribution is recognized. Observe each person's strengths and look for ways to help each one to shine.

3) **Share leadership.** Even where there is a designated leader, every member should take responsibility and share accountability for success. It can be helpful if all members have an opportunity to take the lead when their particular kind of expertise is needed.

4) **Address the desire to belong.** Humans have a fundamental need to be part of communities, particularly those that allow us to make contributions that are appreciated by others. So focus on the power of belonging and find ways to reinforce it. Even silly ways to embrace membership, such as T-shirts or mottoes, can enhance team spirit.

5) **Celebrate little victories.** Team members are most likely to feel satisfied and motivated when they believe they're making progress on meaningful work. To keep up the team energy level, find appropriate ways to celebrate even small wins, such as meeting deadlines or being congratulated by the boss.

6) **Create norms.** Even if leadership is loose, high-performing teams need some structure. For example, when the team conducts group meetings, members should agree on elements such as:

  ◆ Scheduling.

  ◆ Attendance requirements.

  ◆ Promptness.

  ◆ Participation in discussions.

  ◆ Cell phone usage and other interruptions.

  ◆ Ways to track and follow up on action items.

There's no single formula for creating a great team. But a good starting point is to think about a configuration that suits your tasks, allows regular discussion among members, provides a way to acknowledge contributions, and lets everyone enjoy the camaraderie that team membership can bring.

37

Celebrate Your Wins and Theirs

Do you worry so much about what could go wrong that you can't seem to focus on what's going right? If so, you're missing important opportunities.

That was the case with my client Joe*, who led a government branch composed of seven communications specialists. His team had been in place for several years and generally was meeting its goals and coping with constant deadline pressure. The problem, Joe said, was that it felt like his people had "run out of juice." Too often they seemed bored or exhausted, and he was tempted to micromanage in order to prevent mistakes.

We talked about how Joe might restructure the unit's activities not only to deliver more value to the agency, but also to reengage staffers and encourage them to grow. He worked hard to create a new vision for the team, and after a few months built upper management support for a plan to reorganize the branch's responsibilities. The plan dropped several of the team's old projects and added a new one that would require the development of additional skills. After much discussion, Joe's team members welcomed the change and began to seem more enthusiastic about work. But Joe worried that once the group was past the excitement of building something new, the old malaise would quickly return.

At that point, Joe began to tweak his leadership style. In the past, he'd kept careful track of deadlines, and after the team met one target he'd immediately redirect its attention to the next one. This approach kept everything moving, but it seldom allowed people to pause, consider what had gone well, and explore ways to make their work products even better.

Also, by shifting so quickly to the next assignment, Joe had repeatedly missed the ideal time to positively reinforce good work. The most effective time to give feedback is immediately after a task is completed. But Joe tended to save up his praise for each staffer's required annual review. That often left some team members feeling unappreciated or uncertain about whether they were giving Joe what he wanted.

After reading about the importance of a positive work culture, Joe launched a six-month experiment. He promised himself that at least twice each month he would find a way to celebrate his team's good work, or perhaps to draw attention to any good luck. Then, in honor of various accomplishments, he started his new regimen by staging a surprise pizza party, arranging for a big boss to express thanks at an all-hands meeting, and taking individual staffers out for lunch or coffee.

Once he began looking for opportunities to celebrate, Joe found that he was focusing more intently on his team's best efforts. He realized that he'd been taking some high performers' output for granted, because they invariably did so well. He spotted additional ways for staffers to learn from each other's smartest strategies. And, as he involved his customers in some of the team's celebrations, he became more adept at promoting its achievements.

By the end of the six months, Joe was feeling remarkably positive and was committed to celebrating work as part of his leadership brand.

Workplace celebrations can lead to even more success

Celebrations can enhance a positive workplace culture and encourage teams to perform well. Creating a celebration can be a wonderful way to acknowledge achievements and motivate people to continue to excel. Affirmative feedback is a powerful motivator, and a celebratory event is a meaningful way to reinforce an accomplishment. Sharing appreciation for success and good fortune can support the well-being of individuals, foster a sense of community, and promote the health of your whole organization.

If you take note of even modest achievements, it can help you and your colleagues to remain focused on the kinds of details that will lead to further success. Celebrations provide times when coworkers come together, get to know each other better, and develop a shared perspective. Enjoying festive occasions helps workers become friends, and having friends at the office helps you do your best. Arranging celebrations can provide a moment for reflection, allowing people to develop a collective focus on the right stuff. It's a way to direct attention to the organization's goals and values, and to remind participants that they work at a great place.

Of course, the style and magnitude of a celebration should vary with the situation. A few triumphant events may call for a big blowout, but even routine achievements may deserve a brief toast. *Here are 13 ways to celebrate at work:*

1) **Set the meeting tone.** Kick off regular meetings with a brief time to acknowledge recent achievements and thank individuals for their contributions. "Thanks" and "attaboys" can be expressed by the leader or anyone else in the room. A gratitude ritual can set a positive tone and support an atmosphere where it's normal to thank colleagues for what they do.

2) **Arrange a chance to show off.** When your team does well, find an opportunity for members to talk about their activity to senior management or an external audience. If they're shy, you do the talking and let them bask in the glow.

3) **Create an award for overlooked contributions.** Sometimes we stop noticing the people who keep things moving by reliably doing terrific work. Create a Keystone Award and occasionally honor colleagues whose routine excellence is vital to the team effort.

4) **Have a retreat.** Acknowledge the group's importance by taking people out of the office for an event that is about bonding rather than problem solving. Dress casually, share a good meal, and structure activities that allow members to chat casually and have some fun.

5) **Go home early.** If you're the boss, after a big effort, express appreciation by inviting everybody to head out before normal closing time.

6) **Throw a surprise party.** Call an important meeting to ensure everyone will attend; then surprise the employees with a festive event to thank them for a recent success.

7) **Create a media event.** Whether it's a classy video presentation, a picture in the company newsletter, or a photomontage on the bulletin board, honor people for their production by showing it off.

8) **Notice milestones.** People feel more satisfied if they believe they're making progress toward something that counts. So don't wait until the end of a major initiative to celebrate. Express appreciation for key steps along the way. Consider a special lunch party or small gifts to acknowledge the halfway point of a big project. It will help to build enthusiasm for reaching the finish line.

9) **Buy T-shirts.** Even though the items may seem tacky, people often enjoy receiving shirts, paperweights, stuffed animals, and other little gifts decorated with the team logo or slogan. Order T-shirts or mugs for team members who contribute to a stellar effort.

10) **Buy lunch.** It could be a pizza party in the conference room or an elegant meal at a nearby restaurant, but people always like it when you buy lunch. And, during the meal, offer a few heartfelt comments about what you appreciate.

11) **Call on local talent.** Does somebody in your group sing, play an instrument, or do a bit of stand-up? Can you recruit a small group to perform a funny skit? Turn a meeting or pedestrian lunchtime into a party by coming up with some entertainment.

12) **Write notes.** Share a quiet moment of gratitude by taking a few minutes to sit down and write a note to someone who has done well or given you a hand.

13) **Take a break.** To be at your creative best, you should take regular rests. That might include frequent mini-breaks, such as a few minutes of meditation, or it might be longer interludes, such as a couple of hours away from your desk for a massage. When you've completed a tedious or thorny task, celebrate by yourself with a little time off. Even taking a few minutes to chat with a friend can help you to get back to work with new purpose and energy.

Whether it means planning a party for the whole team, or quietly rewarding yourself for taking on a tough task, take time to shine a light on work well done. Even if you're not yet a leader, celebrating gracefully can become a vital part of your flourishing work life and can help you to build a supportive professional community.

38

It's (Usually) Not Okay to Be Late

I dislike being late. It makes me feel anxious and disorganized, and I'm uncomfortable at the prospect of disrupting somebody else's schedule.

On the other hand, I generally don't mind being kept waiting if I'm meeting a friend or client. I always have a book and phone with me, I treat the waiting period as found time, and I catch up on messages or read something I enjoy.

However, there are two conditions to my tolerance. First, I want a heads-up. When I'm not alerted the other person is running late, I worry that I'm in the wrong place, or at the wrong time, or that something awful has happened. Second, I don't want to be made late if it means that I, in turn, will be late for somebody else.

But that's just me. Punctuality can be a surprisingly emotional issue, and attitudes about timeliness vary widely. Some people are angered or insulted if they are kept waiting, believing it shows a lack of respect. Others are annoyed or exhausted by unending demands to stay on schedule.

Flexible attitudes about punctuality can work well where people in a community know what to expect. For example, a 30-minute delay is no problem if everyone in the social group understands that the "seven o'clock dinner" really starts at 7:30.

In the context of your career, however, your standard approach should be to stay on schedule. American business etiquette requires that you show up for meetings and events at the appointed hour. In some organizations the rule is tougher, and to be considered "on time" you must actually arrive a little early. This strict approach to punctuality isn't just an arbitrary tradition. If your lateness causes others to lose minutes of productivity, you've just stolen some of their most valuable resource.

But cultures and expectations vary. In some circles, a fanatical preoccupation with the clock could come across as silly or obnoxious. If you wonder whether you have the right approach to punctuality, look around to see how closely your habits are aligned with those in your environment. *As you ask yourself whether your approach to timeliness is good for your brand, consider these six strategies:*

1) **Know the rules.** The organizations you deal with may have explicit policies about punctuality, but sometimes the general practice is nothing like the policy manual. When you start interacting with a new group, inquire about preferences for meeting start times. Does that 10 o'clock meeting really begin on the hour, or is it considered polite to chat for a few minutes with other attendees?

2) **Bank goodwill.** If you're a person who finds it tough to get to places on time, work hard to be prompt as often as possible. If you can establish a reputation for being punctual, people are more likely to be tolerant when you really can't help being late.

3) **Know the message your behavior sends.** When you're typically late, a colleague may take offense, interpreting your tardiness as an overblown sense of your own importance. On the other hand, if you always make a big deal about starting on the dot, you might come across as intolerant. To be effective, you must understand what your approach to punctuality is saying to those around you. If your lateness says that you just don't care, it's probably time to change your message.

4) **Lighten up.** Getting upset when you're kept waiting is a waste of your energy. The first step in letting go of your negative emotion is to acknowledge that when others are late, it's probably not about *you*; it's a reflection of what's going on in *their* lives. For example, the late arrivers could be struggling with traffic. Instead of fuming, use the waiting time productively or enjoy a quiet moment for reflection.

5) **Respect your team.** If you're a leader, you have a special obligation to stay on time. If you're seldom prompt, the efficiency of the whole group is impacted. And if you are on time for your superiors but not for your direct reports, you're modeling a culture where junior staffers are not respected.

6) **Negotiate the rules.** If you and your colleagues have different views about the value of being punctual, it might be useful to talk. Whether you tend to be tardy, or you're the one who's always kept waiting, you can smooth relationships by forging shared standards of punctuality. It can be helpful for teams to openly discuss questions such as these:

   ◆ Are meeting times a bit flexible, reflecting travel and other uncertainties? For example, is it acceptable to arrive 15 minutes late for a lunch across town? Does the person who travels the furthest get more flexibility?

   ◆ Is it sometimes fine to be really late, such as when the team has to start the weekly meeting without you because the big boss had a question?

   ◆ When is lateness just plain unacceptable, such as when you are having dinner with a client?

   ◆ What's the best way to take the sting out of being late, like giving early notice, apologizing profusely, or doing better next time?

39

Measuring Progress Makes Your Goals Powerful

Throughout this book we discuss how building a resilient career and leading like a CEO require you to stay focused on your goals. Whether you're framing major long-term objectives or simply making your plan for a productive week, how you actually articulate your goals can have an impact on your ability to reach them.

You might start with a general picture of what you want to accomplish. But from there, the way to make your goals truly useful is to decide precisely how you will record and evaluate your headway.

You may have heard about the importance of "measurable goals" more times than you can count. The basic idea is that, in order to keep moving toward your goals, you must come up with specific ways to gauge your progress. For example, if you've always wanted to write a book, a measurable goal could be to write a specific number of words per week. If your book will have about 60,000 words, and you write at least 1,000 words each week, you will come up with a draft manuscript in a little more than a year.

You'll still make progress if you accomplish only a little at a time. As we discussed in Chapter 17, the action steps that move you forward might not be large—they could be as small as sugar grains—but eventually you *will* approach your target if you maintain a steady pace.

I'm sometimes surprised by talented professionals who resist the notion of quantifying their progress. Maybe the concept of metrics strikes them as time consuming, complicated, or boring? Or perhaps they think that some values just can't be counted? ***If you're reluctant to define your goals in measurable terms, consider these four points:***

1) **Measuring creates awareness.** If you regularly count something, you tend to keep it in mind. So if you're working on a new habit, coming up with a metric will help you to keep on the path. For example, many dieticians predict that if you're trying to lose pounds, you're more likely to stick to your diet if you consistently log your food, weigh yourself, and chart your weight. And it's the same for organizations. In businesses, government units, and nonprofits, attention tends to focus on the things that get evaluated and recorded.

2) **Quantity can lead to quality.** When you regularly count your steps, you're likely to take more of them. That's the theory behind fitness tracking devices, like the one I use, the popular Fitbit. And the more you practice an activity, the better you may get at it. My favorite book about the power of practice is Geoff Colvin's *Talent is Overrated.* Colvin examined research about "what really separates world-class performers from everybody else." He concluded that great performers—whether in music, sports, or business—are the ones who practice intensely. Quantity doesn't always produce quality, but often the more times you do something, the more you learn. And when learning is involved, quantity does lead to quality.

3) **Measurement helps build self-control.** "If you can measure it, you can manage it." That quote is often attributed to management guru Peter Drucker, but his take on measurement in the workplace was actually more nuanced. In his great book *Management,* he wrote of the danger that measurement "could be used to control people from the outside and above— that is, to dominate them." He suggested that the better use

of measurement is to "make self-control possible." Drucker thought metrics should be used by every manager "to appraise his own skill and performance and to work systematically on improving himself."

4) **Measurement can replace micromanagement.** As a coach, I've encountered many situations where managers want to delegate but can't seem to do it. Sometimes they hover annoyingly over a project because they want a better sense of how it's going. But when the manager and the project leader are able to come up with the right metrics, suddenly the problem disappears. A good measurement and reporting system can create transparency. That makes it easier both to solve problems and to recognize progress. When you're able to quantify and describe your accomplishments, it's easier for your manager to let go of control.

Explore different types of data and metrics

At times people are slow to create a measurement system because it's not obvious what should be counted. But whereas it's not always easy to quantify the impact or value of your work, grappling with the selection of metrics can contribute to your ultimate success. Choosing your approach to keeping track requires you to ask important questions. The first step may be to break a large goal into smaller pieces. Then you'll want to consider which factors actually matter.

Suppose your New Year's resolution is to get to the office earlier. You start to build a picture by recording your daily arrival times. For two weeks you count how many minutes you arrive before or after the official nine o'clock start time. And then you begin to wonder: Why is it harder to be prompt on some days than on others? So you expand your log to note your bedtime, your hours of sleep, and whether you lay out your next day's clothes before going to bed. You realize that the way to get to work before nine is to go to bed earlier, so you change your evening routine. You start getting out of the house sooner, and your commitment to reach work earlier is reinforced by that little ping of pride each morning when you record your arrival.

It can be useful to experiment a bit as you choose data to show how you're doing. As you explore options, ***consider these three approaches to measuring progress toward your goals:***

1) **Measure progress toward actually completing the mission.**
   Some goals can be framed in numerical terms, which make it
   easy to chart your achievements. Suppose, for example, that you
   want to raise your profile by energizing your blog. It's a simple
   matter to set numerical targets, such as the number of posts you
   intend to publish during the next year.

2) **Count important activities.** Often, things that impact the completion of your mission are beyond your control. In that case,
   observe the things you *can* control. Determine which activities
   are most likely to contribute to your success and start measuring
   them. Let's say your committee wants to raise money for a foundation, but a tough economy means that donors may give less. As
   you think about goals for committee members, identify their most
   important fundraising activities, like calling supporters and meeting with potential donors. A direct measurement approach would
   count output from the members' efforts, like how much money
   they raise each month. But the measure that motivates your team
   could be one that gives credit for their actions—their inputs to the
   process—such as the number of people they call or visit.

3) **Create capacity.** Complex goals may require a phased approach
   to measurement. Often, you can't start racking up actual results
   until you put the tools, systems, and resources in place. If your
   fundraising goal requires something substantial like creating a
   new task-force to raise the money, map the whole process and
   break it into stages. Perhaps your first stage will involve recruiting the task force members, and a key milestone will be the
   initial meeting. In the beginning of your work, the way you evaluate progress will be to monitor the capacity build-out. Once
   your structure is in place, you can shift to more direct measures
   of success, like the number of dollars being raised.

Your wishful thinking can turn into a tangible goal when you describe your
target and start doing things to move you in that direction. Your goal becomes
powerful when you begin to track the things that will help you make progress.

40

Use Those Amazing Checklists

It's wonderful when one simple tool can help you streamline your work and organize your group. That was the case with my client Sarah*, who's an excellent technical writer. Sarah enjoys reporting on complex situations, and she's proud of her ability to present complicated data in a clear way.

Sarah loved her job preparing reports for a large institution, but she felt panic-stricken when she suddenly was made manager of her department. Although Sarah maintained high standards in her own work, she didn't know how to articulate those standards for use by her team members. She said that she wanted them to do excellent work, but she struggled to describe what "excellence" would look like.

During coaching, Sarah decided to put her writing skills to work to assist her team. She drafted detailed checklists as a way to lay out the key elements of three of the group's routine reports. Sarah used the checklists not only to serve as report templates, but also to encourage a dialogue with her writers. First, she invited them to improve her drafts. Then, after the first round of reports was completed, she convened the team to revisit the checklists, evaluate their usefulness, and suggest ways to make them even more help-ful and complete. At the start of her new job, Sarah felt shy about criticizing the work completed by her former peers. But by focusing discussion on the checklists, she was able to establish standards of excellence without making comments that felt personal.

The extraordinary power of checklists attracted public attention in 2007, when the World Health Organization (WHO) urged operating room person-nel to save lives by using one during surgical procedures. The WHO "Surgical Safety Checklist" specifies 19 steps, some as basic as confirming the patient's name and the scheduled procedure. Although all the steps are routine, research showed that without reliance on a checklist, even experienced surgeons might miss at least one step. According to the WHO's Website, a 2009 study found that its surgical checklist "reduced the rate of deaths and serious complications during surgery by more than one-third across all eight pilot hospitals."

The operating room checklist process is much like the procedure that airplane pilots have followed successfully for decades. Proponents say that the aviation checklists not only prevent busy or distracted crews from forgetting steps, but also promote communication and teamwork.

Checklists promote safety, accuracy, and speed

In professions where lives are at stake, protocols increasingly call for checklists because they break complex projects into manageable parts and combat the human tendency to take shortcuts. Checklists are low-tech tools that can also help the rest of us to become more effective. ***Here are examples of ways that you might use checklists to make your work go more smoothly:***

→ **Shape reports.** Use checklists to specify the content, style, and organization of routinely prepared documents.

→ **Assure accuracy.** Whether you are writing or editing, check-lists can promote thorough fact-checking with questions like, "Have you checked the spelling of all names?" and "Are the quotes accurate and properly attributed?"

→ **Organize events.** If you plan meetings, conferences, or par-ties, smooth the process with a comprehensive planning list. Note every possible element, from invitations and RSVPs to the nametags and the menu. After each event, review your standard checklist to make sure that it addressed every development.

→ **Get packing.** Though some checklists include tasks and proce-dures, others simply describe items that you might need. Ease your travel anxieties with a standard list of everything that you might want to take along on a trip.

→ **Consider candidates.** Whether you are hiring an assistant or choosing a service provider, make a list of the skills and exper-tise that matter most to you. It may be easier to make a decision if you use the same checklist to evaluate each option.

→ **Assure best practices.** Checklists can help you avoid mistakes in challenging situations like conducting a difficult staffer's performance review or running the annual meeting. And emer-gency checklists can help you rise to the occasion if the worst occurs, whether the building is on fire or the CEO makes a public relations gaff.

41

Overcome Big Project Letdown

I wasn't surprised when my client Lisa* cancelled our phone meeting because I knew she was completing a big project. Her assignment was to organize a large conference, accompanied by a media blitz, designed to launch a new product for her company.

From what I read online, the conference and all the surrounding hoopla were a success. The activity reached a crescendo on a Friday, and I expected to speak with Lisa during the following week, when I hoped she'd be enjoying a victory lap around the corporate headquarters.

But when we finally spoke, Lisa was on the verge of tears. She couldn't forget the tiny things that had gone wrong, and she worried about people who might be disappointed. On top of that, routine marketing work had piled up during preparation for the product launch and the tall stack of requests now felt daunting. Lisa needed a plan to quickly get through the backlog, but she was reluctant to ask for extra work from her exhausted staff. ***Lisa had a bad case of Big Project Letdown and this is what she felt:***

→ **Exhaustion.** Because the project was so important, Lisa had been working long hours without taking time out for her normal life. At night she was tossing and turning. She'd quit going to the gym, she hadn't spoken with her girlfriends in weeks, and she couldn't remember her last quiet dinner with her husband.

→ **A sense of loss.** Although the project had been rewarding, it had also been invigorating. For its duration she was included with the senior team, and for the first time she spoke frequently with her CEO. And though the pressure was on, her staff rose to the occasion, following her lead and making her proud. Now that the big push was over, everything felt dull and flat. The prospect of tackling overdue routine work felt like drudgery compared to the creative activity involved in the special event.

→ **Depression.** Lisa realized that she was tired and also frustrated at the thought of turning to all the overdue tasks. But she felt so very blue that she was disconcerted. She said, "I know it was a success, so why do I feel so awful? What's wrong with me?"

You can manage Big Project Letdown

Lisa felt better as soon as she realized that it's normal to experience a sense of anticlimax after you've made a big effort. One reason is that during a big push your brain chemistry changes to help keep you going. Perhaps your dopamine spikes in a major meeting, or working with the big boss triggers your serotonin. But when your mood-enhancing chemicals return to their normal levels, it feels like something is wrong with your world.

After taking a day off, Lisa gradually bounced back from her postproject crash. Since then, she has learned to plan ahead to assure a speedy recovery after each major event. *Strategies like these helped Lisa and can help you to avoid or recover from Big Project Letdown:*

→ **Manage expectations.** Part of Lisa's problem was that for weeks she told people, "I'll get back to you right after the conference." So when she came into the office that Monday, a barrage of "can we talk now?" messages made her feel like she was under attack. These days she uses project management software to help make realistic commitments about when her team will fulfill routine requests after a special event is over.

→ **Take breaks.** Lisa's unrelenting pace disrupted the pattern of her life, causing stress at home and in the office, and keeping her awake at night. Now she has learned to keep up her fitness routine and build some quiet time into her schedule. She has found that taking regular brief rests, including quick outdoor walks, can help her stay calm and feeling creative.

→ **Plan ahead.** Lisa is happier if she is looking forward to something. When there was nothing new on the horizon after the conference, the future felt bleak. So now she lines up interesting projects and fun events down the road. By planning activities and vacations far in advance, she always has something to anticipate.

→ **Debrief.** One thing that helped Lisa is that, immediately after the conference, she and her team carefully reviewed what went right and what could be improved in the future. By examining the project details, she had a good understanding of the many things that went well, as well as of ways to be even more successful next time. In the following days, when she had moments of feeling like a failure, she was able to snap herself out of it by remembering the evidence of her success.

→ **Celebrate.** Lisa realized that she probably wasn't the only one who was feeling down in the days after the conference. She wrote notes to the many people who had helped, and she scheduled a festive lunch to thank team members for their hard work. She continued to celebrate by taking her patient husband out to dinner. As she drew other people into her celebration, her satisfaction with the success continued to grow.

It's normal to feel emotional after a significant project or a long-anticipated event. Sometimes the best way to move forward is to notice what you are feeling, and maybe even write about it. And look for ways in which the end of one big project can be transformed into the start of your next one.

42

Know When to Forget about Status

Initially, my friend Robert* was excited when his company offered him an opportunity to move to a different kind of job. He told me that he'd been bored at work for years and the new position could put him on a career track with more interesting opportunities than in his current role. But then he saw the problem. Although the transfer would bring Robert a small bump in pay, it would mean losing his "vice president" title.

I felt sorry for Robert. He had a chance to try something that looked exciting, but he was tortured by the thought that his colleagues would think he was being demoted. And so he was about to decline the offer, even though he was sick of his dull, topped-out VP position.

Soon after Robert and I chatted, I read a compassionate passage in Michael Korda's entertaining book *Horse People*. Writing about the herd behavior of horses, Korda said, "However peaceful horses may look grazing in their fields or dozing solemnly on their feet in their stall, they are always busy, in the sense that their mind is constantly aware of their status, and brooding over anything that might seem likely to change or challenge it. In short, it ain't easy being a horse..."

That's just like Robert and many other people. As social animals, humans may become preoccupied by their status, fretting over anything that challenges it. They might even pass up a wise move because others could regard it as a step down. In short, it ain't easy being human.

Unlike herd animals, however, we don't have to always give in to the pressure from the crowd.

Of course, it's normal to want respect from our colleagues. In his classic theory of human motivation, psychologist Abraham Maslow identified the need for esteem as a basic driver of human behavior. And leaders understand how important it can be for team members to feel accepted and valued by the group.

At work, the desire to look like a winner can keep us hustling when we secretly want to just throw in the towel. And praise and appreciation from our peers can make it all feel worth it once a big effort is over.

But although the desire to move up and look good can bring energy to your career, it also can lead you astray. There are times when the wish for status or accolades can waste your time or lead you to the wrong choices. *Here are five situations when the wiser move may be to let go of your all-too-human yearning for standing or prestige:*

1) **When you're the leader.** Have you worked for a manager who was preoccupied with the trappings of her position? Perhaps she'd insist on an early meeting, but then show up late and play with her phone once the discussion began. Weak leaders may play power games to underscore their high title. Stronger leaders tend to treat everyone with respect, focus on the work, and forget about symbols of rank.

2) **When you get a promotion.** In the first months of a new role, it may be tempting to talk a lot in order to demonstrate your qualifications and knowledge. And it can feel reassuring to show off the power that comes with senior standing. But now that you have the position, be modest about it. Instead, concentrate on listening, learning, and building relationships.

3) **When a job change could bring opportunities.** The idea that your career should keep you moving up some kind of hierarchical ladder is old-fashioned and can be self-destructive. These days, our long professional lives are more complicated and may include lateral shifts and even fresh starts. If you're starting to

feel stuck or insecure on your current track, be open to a change in direction. A short-term loss of grade or title is a small price to pay for a shift that could recharge your professional life. Tell yourself to put aside concerns about what other people think. Eventually, smart observers will recognize a good strategic move.

4) **When you're ready to reinvent yourself.** If you want to smoothly navigate a major work-life transition, the starting point may be your willingness to look like a beginner. I struggled with this when I chose to retire from law and business and start a new career as an executive coach. As an attorney, I drew confidence from my areas of expertise. I had to reframe my thinking before I was comfortable going back to school to learn something new.

5) **When you feel anxious or obsessed.** It's healthy to want respect from others, but self-respect is even more important. If you need public recognition in order to feel good about yourself, it may be time for reflection or counseling. A neurotic need for prestige, or an outsized fear of embarrassment, can make you miserable and jeopardize the success you want so much.

Even if we're not teenagers anymore, we want to look cool. But healthy grown-ups understand that working our way into the "in" crowd is mostly a game. One way to keep your need for prestige under control is by staying in touch with the things that matter to you most in life. Keep focusing on the big picture so it won't be so hard to stop worrying about status symbols when they're holding you back or tripping you up.

And if you're tired of your team members' preoccupation with the petty symbols of their standing, have a little compassion. Fretting too much about rank can be an indicator of pain. Remember: It just ain't easy being human.

43

To Lead without Authority, Know How to Herd Cats

Do you know how to run a committee in a way that gets things done? Or to direct a work group when you don't really have a manager's authority? Much of the work getting done today comes from fostering collaboration among people who don't share identical goals. But whether you're brainstorming a start-up with entrepreneurial pals, chairing a committee, or serving as counsel to a blue ribbon panel, leading folks who don't report to you can be frustrating. It can be like herding cats.

A person who is adept at leading across functional, political, and organizational lines is my friend and longtime mentee Sherry Little. In 2009, Sherry became a founding partner of Spartan Solutions, L.L.C., a company that develops and administers large infrastructure projects. As a result, Sherry often plays a lead role in the creation of public-private partnerships to build things like subway systems, trolley lines, or ferries. Sherry learned political skills as a senior staffer in the U.S. Senate, where crafting transportation legislation required negotiating across party lines. And then, while she was still in her 30s, and before the formation of Spartan, Sherry managed a $6 billion budget as acting administrator of the U.S. Department of Transportation's Federal Transit Administration.

Today, Sherry's work requires her to forge coalitions among people who may have different objectives, interests, and areas of expertise. When I asked her to share her favorite strategies for building an effective committee or task force, **Sherry offered four tips for "herding cats":**

1) **Start strong.** The first meeting of a new group sets the tone for the future. It's vital that the initial meeting, and the invitation process, be smoothly organized. Be sure to structure the discussion and prepare the written materials so that every member leaves with a clear idea of the group's mission.

2) **Allocate tasks.** Make sure every member of the work group is given something specific to do, even if it's minimal. Sherry says that when people don't have even a small assignment, they are more likely to sit back and criticize.

3) **Track action items.** Whether an elected secretary prepares formal minutes or participants take turns e-mailing timely informal notes, it's important to keep track of action items and group decisions. Sherry makes sure that all assignments are put in writing to keep members accountable and on the same page.

4) **Explain decisions.** Regardless of whether you have direct authority, Sherry advises that in a collaborative group, you, as leader, should listen to everybody's views. Then, once you decide upon a course of action, explain the reasoning behind your decision. She says it's particularly important to describe how you took contrary opinions into account. When team members understand and respect the process, they will feel valued. Furthermore, Sherry says, they'll be more likely to go along with your decision this time, and to participate positively in the next debate.

Use the "Herding Cats Triangle" to plan your strategy

As Sherry knows, leading a collaborative effort requires a mix of strong organizational skills and softer skills, such as recognizing what each person needs and wants. In talking with clients, I often use a little model I call the "Herding Cats Triangle" to help work out a leadership strategy for a team or committee. The model, which consists of three questions, is loosely inspired by the "Strategic Triangle" described by Mark Moore in his book *Creating Public Value*. ***If leading your group does feel like herding cats, keep things moving ahead by regularly running through these three questions:***

1) **What's the mission?** It's important for all participants to understand why the group exists. That doesn't mean that goals can't evolve with time, but the members must always have a shared, clear view of their collective purpose and responsibilities. If the committee or team is part of a larger organization, be sure your activities are consistent with the bigger vision. And, as you look at a specific project or challenge, define the likely deliverables and structure them so they support the organizational mission.

2) **Who are the stakeholders and what do they need?** As a starting point, learn as much as possible about all group members, including what they want from their membership and what interest sectors they represent. The more you know about the needs and interests of participants, the easier it will be for you to foster cooperation and compromise. Beyond the immediate participants, think about the interests of other possible stakeholders, because they have the potential to offer support or limit your progress. Regularly consider whether additional groups and individuals might be interested in or impacted by the group's activities.

3) **Are the right meeting logistics in place?** Running productive meetings is a key part of your job as leader. To start, make sure that you have the necessary capacity for tasks such as distributing the agenda and minutes, and keeping track of assignments. Chapter 31 describes more techniques for structuring meetings to keep your group moving forward.

To lead a relatively unstructured group, you must be highly organized. At the same time, you should recognize that, to some degree, participation in the effort is voluntary. That requires you to pay attention to every participant and be sensitive to the way each person is likely to be motivated.

44

How Bigger Goals Can Take You Further

When I first met Gayle Williams-Byers in the early 90s, I was impressed by her determination. At the time, she had begun a coveted internship in the White House. She was supposed to be writing a paper about her learning experience as an intern, for 12 hours of academic credit from Case Western Reserve University, where she was a junior.

Gayle's problem was that the only assignment her White House bosses had given her was to make photocopies. She needed those credit hours, but she didn't feel she'd be able to claim them because she wasn't learning anything.

Gayle found her way to my Washington office through an acquaintance. She requested a few minutes of my time, then pretty much announced that she'd be transferring her internship to my team at Consolidated Natural Gas Company. She said that she'd do anything, that she'd make it worth my while to take her on, but that she needed a challenge and she absolutely had to learn something.

Today, both of Gayle's parents have PhDs, but when she was growing up, no one in her family had attended college. And as one of her family's first college students, Gayle was anxious to learn as much as possible. She regarded the semester in Washington as the opportunity of a lifetime, important not just to her, but also to her extended family. She wanted a full experience, even if it meant walking away from the White House and inventing something new.

Gayle returned to my office after graduation and kept working for the company while completing a joint JD/MPA program. Then, during her last years in D.C., she was counsel to a Senate committee. In her early 20s, Gayle encountered many challenges, from racism to breast cancer, but I never doubted her ultimate success. I knew she wouldn't quit hustling to develop her potential because her future meant so much to her supporters.

During a 2011 Kwanzaa celebration, a community group in the Cleveland suburb of South Euclid gave Gayle a Kujichagulia Award to honor her self-determination. That was just one of the celebrations that followed her election, at age 37, as South Euclid's first African American municipal court judge.

I agree with Gayle's neighbors that she is a model of self-determination, and I'm so proud of her. She has always kept pushing toward her goals, even when life seems to have stacked the odds against her. A low point came during her election campaign, when she was going door-to-door, talking about her plan to bring change to the South Euclid Municipal Court system.

At the first house on a long street, an angry man refused to listen to her pitch. He jabbed her with his finger saying, "We don't want to hear it. We've already made up our minds. You got no chance, kid." Gayle was tired. She looked down the row of about 30 houses and thought, "I don't think I can do this again."

Her candidacy was a long shot and Gayle almost gave up. I asked her why she didn't. She said, "That's what self-determination is. You dig really deep when you don't want to, and you decide to take one more step toward your goal."

Gayle shares her parents' belief that, no matter how humble your beginning, you can become just about anything you want. She says, "If you can imagine it, you can do it." The most important thing to know is that "it's easier to keep going when you have a goal that's bigger than yourself."

For her judicial race, Gayle developed a comprehensive plan for a more transparent, service-focused court. And when she felt discouraged, she tried to stay focused on what the change could mean for her community. I've often seen the same thing with my clients. Having a vision about something important to a community makes you feel powerful and energetic, whereas personal ambition alone might just make you anxious. ***Here are six suggestions from Judge Gayle on building an outsized career:***

1) **Define big goals.** Look for ways that you can contribute to or create change for a broader group, not just for you. Identify a mission—for your team, family, or community—that will get your juices flowing. If you feel like you're too busy to worry about a larger mission, ask yourself why your job matters so much. Are you working this hard for your family? Or perhaps because you believe in what you're doing? You are more likely to persevere once you realize that more than your own ego is already at stake.

2) **Control what you can control and work to accept the rest.** When Gayle had cancer during law school, she faced difficulties that she couldn't change. But she focused her energy on studying hard and on taking care of herself. She says she couldn't control the fact of having cancer, but her "gift from cancer" was that she learned to control how she spent her time.

3) **Find mentors and role models.** Gayle deeply respects her parents and continues to learn from them. And, as I know well, she has never been shy about recruiting other mentors. She says that it is easier to keep going in the tough times if you've built yourself a cheering squad. And with practice, you get better at asking for help.

4) **Act like you have self-discipline.** Do you sometimes think about how much you could accomplish if only you were more disciplined? Gayle suggests that you identify the steps you would take toward your goal if you did in fact have that necessary self-discipline. For example, to start turning in your weekly report by the noon Friday deadline, would you draft it before leaving work on Thursday? Once you have a vivid picture of what you'd do if only you were more disciplined, start acting like that. Work on your report on Thursday afternoons. And each time you decide to "act like that" you'll exercise your self-discipline "muscle" and build your self-control.

5) **Laugh at yourself.** There's a danger that self-determination can morph into arrogance or self-righteousness. A good way to avoid that trap is to keep your sense of humor, particularly when it comes to your own failures and mistakes. Gayle says she looks pretty silly when she walks around her community in her sweats at 5:30 in

the morning, hand delivering "door-knockers" to inform citizens about how to access the resources of their court system.

6) **Build your confidence.** A powerful career aimed at big goals requires a good deal of self-confidence. One way to become surer of yourself is to define and achieve a series of small goals. Each time you reach one little target, you'll feel a bit stronger and you'll gradually become ready to aim for larger targets. Meanwhile, try to keep acting *as if* you were confident.

When you contemplate your long-term goals, it can seem presumptuous to feel passionate about making the world a better place. You might think, "How can I make that kind of difference, with my puny skills and resources?" To get past that kind of thinking, imagine what your goals could be if you *were* a smarter, braver, more confident person. What would you aim for, if you were an extraordinary person like Judge Gayle? Well—here's the secret: You *are* an extraordinary person, just like Judge Gayle. What you need to do is to imagine those big goals, then get started, even if you move forward just one sugar grain at a time.

45

You Might Hesitate,
but Keep Going

This chapter explores an issue that seems to impact a disproportionate number of women: Why do so many talented professionals hesitate to reach for major career opportunities when the time seems right? I've heard executives worry about how often their female star performers seem reluctant to go after a higher job. And I've heard clients struggle with that tendency in their own behavior. Some never feel quite ready to step up, even when they see less-qualified men successfully moving into leadership.

In recent years public conversations have asked why, in at least some fields, so many talented women appear reluctant to go after the plumb jobs. Particularly in areas like law and technology, why aren't women moving to the top of the hierarchy at the same pace as their male colleagues?

The discussion about this phenomenon doesn't seem to be an us-against-them, women-versus-men thing. I've heard insightful men express concern that too few women are reaching their full professional potential. For example, two male professors recently asked me why their outstanding female business students seem to have lower job aspirations than their less-qualified male classmates. And I've heard some of the most accomplished American journalists—men and women—talk about how leading print and digital newsrooms are still dominated by a male culture, despite the fact that university journalism programs often have more women than men students.

Part of the problem may be lodged in the workplace culture resulting from the experiences of early women to enter many professions. When I joined the first big wave of women moving from law schools to Washington law firms, it was wonderful and exciting. But at times being a "first woman" was frightening. Even where there was no hazing or explicit double standard, it could be exhausting and bewildering to join all-male teams.

Many "old girls" who fought for professional acceptance decades ago, and who went on to success after success, say they still feel scarred. And these highly accomplished women still experience surprising flashes of uncertainty when they know it's time to seize an opportunity. In some cases it feels like exhaustion; it gets tiring to keep pushing when it feels like the odds are against you.

Notice your hesitation and adjust your timid behavior

Do you experience an unreasonable reluctance to step up when, intellectually, you know it's time to reach for the opportunity you've worked so hard to get? Your hesitant behavior may not be an isolated response that holds you back only when it's time for your big career move. If you look closely, you may see that it's part of a broader behavior pattern—a pattern that you can elect to change.

If you practice managing your hesitancy in small moments, you'll learn to deal with it more effectively in the face of bigger challenges and opportunities. *Here are little ways your uncertainty may show up, and strategies you can use to get past it:*

→ **Self-deprecating speech.** Some people undercut their otherwise professional presence, and their own feeling of confidence, by repeatedly using overly modest phrases such as "I'm probably wrong, but . . ." when a simple statement would be stronger. If that sounds like you, pause before saying, "I think perhaps it might be a good idea to try X." Instead, practice saying, "Let's do X."

→ **Excessive risk aversion.** When they first had access to law, engineering, and finance degrees, female students were sometimes mocked or intimidated. This exacerbated academic and job pressures, causing some women to grow less sure of themselves and, eventually, become overly fearful of career risks. Regardless of the underlying cause, and whether you're male or female, do you think that your outsized concern about the potential for failure might somehow be holding you back at work? If you know that you're more risk averse than your average colleague, you can choose to manage the way you approach opportunities. Imagine how you would act if you *didn't* feel so tentative. Now, look for occasions to practice acting more like *that*.

→ **Apologizing.** Feeling unwelcome at work may have been why some women started saying "sorry" even when they weren't at fault. It was tempting to blame themselves when things weren't going well. For some, it's still a challenge to face problems quickly and move the conversation on to solutions. Chapter 25 has suggestions about when to get over your urge to say "sorry."

→ **Dithering.** That hesitant feeling can leave you frozen, caught between staying or going, like the proverbial donkey between two handfuls of straw. Often, the worst decision is the one you don't really make. If you feel like you can't make up your mind, you might be better off tossing a coin than agonizing endlessly. Give yourself a time limit on decision-making. Choose one of the options even if your choice feels arbitrary. And move forward decisively, whatever you decide.

Notice your hesitation and move on anyway

Successful dieters know you don't have to eat just because you're hungry.

When you feel a little pang of hunger, instead of reaching for the cookie jar, you can elect to take a deep breath and just ignore that urge to munch. It can be the same when you have a sudden pang of inadequacy. You *don't* have to react just because of a little momentary discomfort. If you simply notice your feeling of hesitation and act anyway, your uncertainty may soon pass.

It helps to recognize that each of us—male or female—experiences fear at times. And it's normal to pause when we're facing an unfamiliar situation. But just because you experience a twinge of uncertainty doesn't mean you have to remain immobile. Once you've assessed the obstacles, you have the option to *act* like a confident person and forge ahead.

46

Ageism Is Real: Deal With It Sooner than Later

While finishing her MBA at a top tier university, Sarah* was aggressively recruited by a large company. She accepted their offer to join the marketing department. Once there, she connected with a powerful mentor who helped her snag plum assignments. For several years Sarah was the most junior professional in her group, and she enjoyed being treated like a young star.

But then the growing company made a wave of new hires and Sarah began to feel neglected. She felt stuck with the routine work, while the more interesting new projects went to her younger colleagues.

Sarah was asked to supervise the internship program, but she told me she didn't enjoy the work. She said the interns didn't have the right work ethic and were obsessed by technology. And one day, as she entered the office kitchen, she heard them making fun of her for being clueless about the power of social media.

When Sarah came to coaching, she complained that she was past her career peak. She felt like she was cut off from the company's high potential challenges and might be too old to compete for another good job elsewhere. Sarah was 34 at the time.

Sarah believed she was struggling with age discrimination and to some degree her concerns were well founded. Ageism is rampant in the workplace and can be hard to fight. And even 30-somethings like Sarah can find themselves sidelined by employers seeking fresh talent.

To improve her situation, Sarah found ways to demonstrate energy and enthusiasm. And soon she worked her way out of her slump. One thing that helped her was finding examples of older professionals whose age did not seem to limit their success. She noticed that whereas some coworkers were dissed for being out of date, these others seemed timeless despite their years.

Try these strategies for overcoming ageism

If you're facing subtle age bias at work and you want to stay where you are, you need to come up with a plan. A starting point for getting past ageism is to understand the negative stereotypes on which it's based. Then make it clear that the stereotypes don't fit you. ***Consider these seven strategies for avoiding the burden of age discrimination:***

1) **Be tech savvy.** You don't have to *enjoy* sharing on Instagram, Skyping, or building a Twitter community. But if those are the ways that your colleagues or customers communicate, you need to participate. If you want to stay in the game, keep up with the technology. Take classes or find help to buy the devices you need and do whatever it takes to keep your skills current. And when you don't understand the latest developments, avoid the temptation to indulge in a Luddite rant. Express an interest, ask for assistance, and get on board.

2) **Look and act fit.** Some employers and younger workers believe that their older colleagues may have physical limitations that will prevent them from performing their fair share of the work. And your boss or clients won't offer you new challenges if they think you are about to have a heart attack. If you want to maximize your career options, it is vital not only that you stay healthy but that you also *look* healthy and exude energy.

3) **Talk healthy.** Most of us have health issues from time to time, but we can manage the way they impact us in the workplace. As

we mentioned in Chapter 19, it's possible to sabotage yourself by talking too much about your symptoms or crises. If you endlessly discuss your health challenges, not only will you sound boring, but people may start to think of you as frail and over the hill. Talk about the great hike you took last weekend instead of how sore you felt on Monday morning.

4) **Be stylish.** Looking shabby may seem cool when you're 22. But the older you get, the more important it is to look polished and up to date. If your clothes, hairdo, or glasses seem out of style, you may seem like you are past your prime. That doesn't mean you should dress like a kid, but you should aim for a look that feels current.

5) **Don't bring up your age.** If you are older—or younger—than the people you work with, it is very tempting to keep mentioning that fact. But if you can refrain from alluding to the age difference, chances are your coworkers will forget about it. And avoid reminding people of your age by endlessly telling stories about the good old days.

6) **Build a varied network.** If you are accustomed to hanging out with friends of all ages, you are more likely to blend easily into a group of younger or older workmates. If you don't allow age to be a barrier in your social life, you will be more comfortable talking and keeping up with different age groups at the office.

7) **Listen to your colleagues.** A great starting point for building strong relationships at work is to genuinely listen to what other people have to say. If you're part of the older set, show an interest in what younger colleagues say and learn from their perspective.

If you put aside your own prejudices about age and look for opportunities to work on projects with people of all generations, you'll become more skillful at avoiding age bias.

47

How to Stay Steady When Change Is Constant

A longtime mentee, Andrea Wilkinson, asked me to give a talk about how to survive in an organization that's going through a multiyear transition. Andrea is an executive who leads global government affairs initiatives to launch strategies for biopharmaceutical products and she wanted me to speak to group of women in her industry.

But when I heard the topic, I was surprised. That's because I can't think of anybody more skillful than Andrea at navigating a satisfying career through an industry experiencing prolonged change. She has survived multiple mergers, division liquidations, and company restructurings. And, from the time she was a young congressional staffer, Andrea has been adept at jumping ship at the right time, making perfect landings and always creating goodwill along the way.

Then I realized that Andrea didn't have questions herself, but was concerned about her industry colleagues. She saw some of them worrying and frozen with anxiety, instead of hustling to come up with her kind of survival strategies. So in preparing my remarks, I used Andrea as a model for thriving in the midst of uncertainty and transition. *Here are Andrea's tips for steering a steady career course even when the environment gets stormy:*

→ **Know that it's not about you.** Organizational change is like a torrential rain storm. It's pouring everywhere, not just on you. Complaining won't help and bitterness can make your situation worse. It's vital to job survival that you look at the big picture and focus on the future. Let go of any anger at finding yourself in a game you didn't sign up for, and concentrate on playing the cards you've been dealt.

→ **Understand your industry and its environment.** One reason Andrea keeps landing on her feet is that she always puts in the time to understand her company's business, as well as the surrounding market, regulatory framework, and political situation. She knows a lot about the competition, she's alert to the needs and interests of customers, and she's well informed about the winds of innovation. By thinking like a CEO, Andrea can spot the trends and be ready when the next wave hits.

→ **Know your bosses' goals.** Your longtime supervisor may fondly recall your contributions from a few years back, but that's probably not enough to save you when the going gets tough. Your most valued colleagues are the ones solving today's problems and contributing to the achievement of tomorrow's goals. If you want to do well in the coming months, be sure you understand your bosses' immediate objectives. Ask yourself: what do they need in order to be successful? And are there more ways I can help them succeed?

→ **Network! Network! Network!** One reason Andrea does so well is because she is so widely connected. She makes friends wherever she goes, she keeps in touch even when she's busy, and she's always willing to offer help or ask for it when she needs it. As we've discussed throughout this book, whether you are looking for a new job or a new idea, your position will be stronger if you have a broad network. Andrea urges that you take the time to listen when you meet someone, join groups, volunteer for projects, and find other ways to get to know people throughout your organization and beyond it.

→ **Find stability in other places.** Some folks are less at ease with uncertainty than others. If the constant state of change at work is getting you down, find people and communities to rely upon in other aspects of your life. Although she can be a bit of a workaholic, Andrea is smart about building a balanced life. She is active in her church, she works hard to stay connected with many friends, and she finds the time to visit widely scattered family members, as well as mentors like me. Andrea has created structures in her life that give her a place to rest when everything at work seems crazy.

→ **Be in great shape.** Let's face it: Change can be exhausting. When the world seems to be shifting, it takes extra energy just to get through the basics. So, although working around the clock might be the answer in an emergency, it's a shortsighted strategy when transition is the new normal. You need sustained energy for the long haul. Andrea is not an athlete, but she has learned that a regular fitness routine and enough sleep are critical to strong performance during difficult times.

→ **Reduce financial pressures.** One thing that has helped Andrea keep her jobs is that she has never become desperate at the thought of losing one. For a while she dreamed of buying a larger home, but instead she's held onto her little stone house and diversified her investments. When times are uncertain, it's wise to build up your rainy day fund or lay the groundwork for alternative sources of income. And there could be another benefit to pursuing some sort of entrepreneurial sideline. I've noticed that when clients start a side gig, whether it's consulting or a part-time job, it sometimes brings new energy to their day job. Creating your small business can inspire your entrepreneurial thinking and refresh your career enthusiasm.

48

Art Can Boost Your Creativity at Work

As a resilient, entrepreneurial professional, you must be able to change with changing circumstances and constantly find ways to make your work product a bit more valuable. And that requires you to be innovative—to be always open to learning and willing to create something new. But it's difficult to innovate when you're exhausted.

So how can you be at your creative best when your workload is already overwhelming? The answer is this: To do your best work you *must* stay in shape, physically, emotionally, and spiritually. You already know that a key to flourishing is to commit to your health and fitness program, which will support all aspects of your life. But that's just the starting point. One way to stimulate your innate creativity, and promote your well-being at the same time, is to engage with art.

Merry Foresta, an expert on American art, is the author of numerous books, including two in 2015: *Artists Unframed*, which features spellbinding snapshots of legendary artists; and *Irving Penn, Beyond Beauty*, featuring 161 of the great photographer's iconic images.

As an art historian and curator, Merry has long been fascinated by the relationship between art and innovation. For example, in studying the 19th century she was intrigued by the rich contributions of artist/scientists like Samuel Morse. He was one of America's great painters and then went on to invent the telegraph; and for good measure he also introduced photography to this country. Morse was prolific, but his combination of interests wasn't unusual in his circles. According to Merry, up until the 20th century, studying art was one of the ways that leaders were educated and encouraged to develop critical thinking.

For more than three decades, I've enjoyed learning from my friend Merry and brainstorming with her about ways to encourage innovation. Our first big project together was in the early 90s when Merry was curator of photography for the Smithsonian Institution's American Art Museum and I was leading external affairs for the Consolidated Natural Gas Company. At that time, the Smithsonian had rarely partnered with a company, but we worked through the institutional concerns and came up with a new collaborative model. The result was a CNG Collection of Photography at the Smithsonian, including a lovely book and a series of exhibitions.

Merry's final role as a full-time Smithsonian executive was to create its groundbreaking Photography Initiative, an online entrance to the Institution's vast collection of photographs. These days, while occasionally serving as a guest curator, Merry works with museums, universities, and other organizations in new ways. They call her when they want to reexamine their assumptions and foster innovation in their programs. Along the way, Merry helps clients rediscover that art can inspire original thinking, allow people to make new connections among complex issues, and inspire them to achieve in satisfying new ways.

Merry uses the now-popular term "Creative Culture" to describe a workplace or other environment where, she says, "creative ideas are encouraged, supported, protected, and nurtured for further development, until their true value can be understood and appreciated. Creativity brings imagination, curiosity, experimentation, and idea sharing into all manner of daily activities. And Creative Culture can bring imagination, diversity, curiosity, experimenting, and idea sharing into our work."

One path to fostering an organization's Creative Culture is to provide access to art, whether it means sponsoring a field trip or installing artworks throughout the office space. "Even the language of art resembles the language of innovative leadership," Merry says. "Art is often about surprise, finding a new perspective, seeing things we had never before noticed, developing a vision, and communicating that vision with others. So is leadership."

"By engaging in art, or simply looking at art," Merry says, "we see new things, make new connections, and learn that it is fine to ask questions and push boundaries. Some businesses are leading the way, using art to encourage employees to break out of their limited thinking and invent new ideas."

In the last year or so, Merry has been particularly intrigued by the concept of spending more time with fewer things as a way to experience art in a profound way. The idea was introduced by Peter Clothier in his 2012 book, *Slow Looking*, and is now gaining attention at a number of museums that see this approach as a way to more deeply engage their audiences.

Merry describes the concept as "an antidote to contemporary life." Often, when busy people visit a museum they dash through, glancing at as many works of art as they possibly can. The "slow art" alternative approach might start with 30 minutes of strolling from room to room, but then the viewer would return to a favorite painting and study it for the next half hour.

"Sometimes you're rewarded more than you might have thought possible if you're able to deeply look and consider a single painting over a longer period of time. As you contemplate it minute after minute, you begin to draw conclusions and gather ideas about art and perhaps even about creativity itself," Merry says.

It's not clear why long, deep looking can be so transformative, but one theory is that it becomes a form of meditation. "This kind of viewing can change your patterns of thought. It fosters your ability to get out of your rut, and think in entirely different ways," Merry says.

Refresh creativity by engaging with art

If you want to bring new creativity to your team, or simply to your own work, one way to begin is by looking at art. *Consider these strategies for stimulating innovation through art:*

- **Do some team building.** Instead of your normal quick lunch, arrange with colleagues to visit a local art museum. Encourage people to get to know each other better by talking about what they like and don't like. Merry says, "There is no such thing as 'good' or 'bad,' just 'intriguing' and 'interesting'!" Discussing exhibits can be a great way to bridge cultural, age, and other gaps.

→ **Try "slow looking."** Find a piece of art you like and study it for 20 or 30 minutes. At first, it may seem that you can't stay still for so long, but as you continue to focus, you'll begin to see more and more.

→ **Try another type of museum.** Merry says that whether you're in the butterfly gallery at the Natural History Museum in Washington, or viewing the collection of First Ladies' gowns in the nearby American History Museum, you can find art and beauty in almost any kind of exhibition. So if your group is turned off by the idea of an "art" museum, try another kind of exhibit.

→ **Redefine your book club.** Do you belong to a book club or some other kind of social group? Vary your regular program by suggesting that one meeting be scheduled at a local museum.

→ **Take a course.** Museums are finding new ways to engage and educate their patrons, and many schools and universities offer continuing education programs touching upon the arts. Stimulate your creative self by taking a course or signing up for a workshop.

→ **Take art home.** Museum stores offer postcards and posters that make it possible to take home exciting art at a reasonable price. And, of course, the Web makes it possible for us all to look at art, no matter where we live or work.

49

The Right Way to Move On

Most smart professionals understand the importance of getting off to a great start in a new job. But some don't take full advantage of that other opportunity in a transition: the chance to tie up loose ends in the old job and turn the experience into a building block for the future.

Bill* is a young lawyer who was let go from his law firm after the leaders of his energy group left the partnership, taking their clients with them. Bill started his week as an associate with a bright future, but by Friday he was ushered out of the office with a small severance payment and a cardboard carton of personal items.

Bill was stunned and then angry. However, on the advice of a mentor, he controlled his emotions and quickly launched a plan that paid off later. Bill saw that the firm's senior lawyers were furious with the departing energy group and associated him with the traitors, even though he hadn't been invited to join their new enterprise. And he recognized that he'd been unwise during his time at the firm in not making an effort to get to know colleagues outside the busy energy practice. Most worrisome, he feared that former colleagues who weren't his friends would describe him as not competent enough to either stay in the firm or be invited to join the departing unit.

Determined to make the best of his situation, Bill launched a process that changed the way his former firm remembered him and ultimately led to a new job. In the days after his departure, he methodically contacted the law firm leaders and staff and found ways to thank each of them for something. Even though it often felt like a reach, he wrote notes expressing appreciation for the collegial atmosphere, the training in managing client accounts—for any kindness or strength he could describe without being insincere. And as a few years went by, he found ways to stay in touch, even referring a little business to a friend in the old firm.

What Bill did so well was reframe his law firm experience in the minds of his former colleagues. Most of them probably didn't remember him vividly, but now they did think of him positively. This was reflected in the fact that they occasionally sent him energy work they could no longer handle. And when they eventually decided to rebuild the firm's energy capability, they remembered Bill and recruited him to rejoin, this time as a partner.

Use these strategies for a departure that will pave your way in the future

Whether you're sad to go or can't wait to get out the door, it's normal in a career transition to focus more on the future than on the past. But if you're smart, you'll do what it takes to create a classy departure. In today's fluid job market, it's inevitable that you'll bump into some of these people again. And, when that happens, what they may remember is your last few days on the job. *Here are five tips for leaving your job the right way:*

1) **Give proper notice.** Once you've decided to accept another opportunity, tell your boss immediately, before word gets around. The boss may not like being surprised by your departure, but it'll be much worse if the news drifts in through the grapevine. Give as much notice as possible—two weeks or a month is common, but more could be better. And follow up your conversation with a very brief resignation letter that clearly states your last day on the job.

2) **Resist the urge to speak up.** You may have fantasized about how great it would feel to tell the team what you really think. Don't

do it! Your goal now is to end things on a good note, not point out the error of their ways. Even formal exit interviews should be approached with caution because you can't really count on confidentiality.

3) **Finish your work and leave a trail.** Your last days on the job are a great time to show that you have what it takes. If you can't complete your projects, leave them in good shape so the next person will know where to get started. Write notes about your tasks, contacts, and responsibilities to help your coworkers or your replacement keep things moving. If you leave things in a mess, that's how they'll always think of you.

4) **Say "thanks."** Think about every person, at every level, who has been helpful to you in some way. Don't dramatize. But write notes, stop by your colleagues' desks, or find other appropriate ways to thank them for what they have done or what they have meant to you. The more specific you make your "thank you's," the more effective and appreciated they will be.

5) **Make plans to stay in touch.** Make sure everybody has your new contact information and confirm that you have theirs. If you haven't connected with them on LinkedIn, do it now. You're likely to see many of these people again, but don't leave it all to chance. Think about the people you most want in your future and promise yourself that you will find ways to make it happen.

In a career market where people change jobs frequently, knowing how to say "goodbye" with grace has become an important skill. An essential part of your smooth transition is treating each one of your old colleagues as though they still matter.

50

Choose to Be an Optimist

During my second year of law school, I hit a low point. I was exhausted from long hours of work and feeling sorry for myself because I was paying my way through school. And somehow I got it in my head that I wouldn't be able to find a good job after graduation. I dragged through, day after day, with a little voice in my head saying, "I'll never get a job. I'll never get a job."

Then my sister Helen reported that a routine exam had shown our brother Dick to have a tumor on his spine. Helen, a nurse, said the spine was a dangerous place for a tumor and if it were malignant, Dick might not have long to live. Dick was rushed immediately into surgery. Happily, we soon heard the good news that the lump was just a harmless cyst, and Dick was in no danger.

The next morning I woke up in a wonderful mood. My career worries had drifted away, I was confident that things would work out, and life felt good.

Then I noticed: My life was no different than it had been the day before Helen's call. But my depression had lifted and I once again felt confident and ready to face the world. The scare about Dick's health had pulled me out of my self-pity and given me a chance to focus on the big picture.

So I wondered: If a momentary scare could shake me out of my pessimism, shouldn't I be able to do that for myself? I knew I was born a worrier, but I decided that from then on I'd make better choices about whether to let my worries take over my life.

I experimented with various ways of holding my pessimism in check, like refocusing on the bigger picture and talking back to the voice in my head. And I found that when I kept an optimistic outlook, my career did indeed tend to flow smoothly. Years later, I came across a book that helped me understand that I was on the right track. I was captivated by *Learned Optimism: How to Change Your Mind and Your Life* by leading psychologist Martin E.P. Seligman.

Often called "the father of Positive Psychology," Dr. Seligman has spent years studying "well-being" and ways that normal people can choose to become happier and more fulfilled in life. Reading his work reinforced my own belief, developed through trial and error, that optimism is a choice and we don't have to be controlled by our innate tendency toward pessimism.

Practice techniques for choosing optimism

Optimism is a positive attitude that carries with it an expectation that things will probably work out for the best. A growing body of research from multiple disciplines suggests that optimism can set you up for career success, improve your social life, help you overcome stress and many kinds of difficulties, and support your efforts to stay healthy.

Pessimism, on the other hand, can undercut your level of achievement, weaken your immune system, and make it more likely that you'll become depressed. In the workplace, pessimism is valuable in performing tasks that require an awareness of risks, such as drafting legal documents. Even for lawyers, however, a pessimistic style can be a burden when it's time to woo clients or manage projects. Generally, it's the optimists who enjoy more fruits of success.

Some lucky optimists are just born that way, but the rest of us need not despair. Dr. Seligman documented that you can build optimism by modifying your internal dialogue. The trick is to recognize and dispute your pessimistic thoughts. For example, if you catch yourself thinking "I'll never get this right," you can argue back to yourself that you're just starting out and will get much better with practice.

In my own life, and working with clients, I've seen good results using these techniques pioneered by Dr. Seligman:

→ **Catch that thought.** Learn to identify self-defeating thoughts that automatically run through your mind, particularly when you're feeling down or discouraged. Simply noticing your frequent negative attitudes—such as, "I'm so bored" or "This will never work out"—will help to tame them.

→ **Argue back.** As we discussed in Chapter 7, you can talk back to the voice in your head. Once you observe a negative refrain, dispute it, just as you would in conversation with a dear friend who was putting herself down. If you notice a voice saying, "I'm a loser," respond with something like, "You have what it takes to start winning."

→ **Test the accuracy.** One simple way to dispose of a pessimistic thought is to demonstrate that it's just not true. Look to external evidence, and then dismiss exaggerated statements such as, "I always fail at things like this."

→ **Find other explanations.** Most situations have many causes, but pessimists tend to cling to the worst possible options. They may leap to the most permanent and pervasive explanation imaginable, such as, "I'm just too old to do this." Dispute negativity by proposing alternative explanations, like: "Maybe I didn't prepare enough this time, but I can do better next time."

Here are more suggestions for developing a more optimistic approach to life:

→ **Make lists.** Carry around a small notebook in which to list each negative phrase that plays repeatedly inside your head. Periodically review the list and create a new list by reframing each pessimistic thought into a positive statement. For example, "I'm too fat," may become "Today I will eat consciously" on the new list. Read the positive list at least daily.

→ **Appreciate the good stuff.** You can generate a surge of optimism by refocusing your attention on the more positive aspects of any situation. For example, if you're frustrated with the stresses of your job, look at the total picture and list five things you appreciate about your professional life. Review the list frequently.

→ **Make goodwill deposits.** Each time you say something kind or positive to another person, or go out of your way to do a good deed, there will be at least two impacts. First, it will be as though you've made a deposit in an account where that person can store up positive feelings about you. And you'll know that the goodwill might come in handy in the future. Second, your positive gesture toward another person will probably provide a lift in your own attitude.

→ **Resist naysayers.** Sometimes that negative dialogue isn't all in your head. Pessimistic people can drain your energy and pull whole groups off track. Avoid negative people when you can and try not to let them bring you down when their company is unavoidable. When you must deal with angry or disrespectful clients or coworkers, try to summon up a feeling of compassion for their angst. Then observe your negative emotions stimulated by their attitude or behavior, and imagine that you are opening your heart and letting those feelings float away.

→ **Talk to people.** Pessimists may isolate themselves when facing difficulties, which can make things worse. When things aren't going well, resist your urge to curl up in a hole. Instead, seek ways to enjoy even small positive connections with other people. If things are troublesome in one sector, like work, find new energy and renewed optimism by structuring happier interactions in other parts of your life.

→ **Plan for the worst.** If you have a strong pessimistic streak, you naturally start thinking about all the things that could go wrong. If you're worrying about developments that are out of your control, remind yourself that there's no point in torturing yourself when there's nothing you can do. But when you're thinking about things that are within your span of control, your best bet may be to create a contingency plan. When you have a worst case plan in place, it's easier to shift your focus away from your worries.

→ **Smile.** If you put on a happy face and act like an optimist, you're likely to actually experience an emotional lift. And the upswing in your mood may continue to build when other people return your smile.

→ **Spend time in nature.** There's growing evidence that spending time outdoors can help you to overcome moderate depression, particularly if you walk or engage in other active pastimes. I've had many clients who've found a daily walk to be helpful in keeping up their positive outlook.

→ **Get help.** If your anxiety feels out of control or you always wake up grouchy, it may be time to seek professional help. Many kinds of therapy can help you to tackle your depression and rediscover your optimism. For example, cognitive behavioral therapy—including emerging online versions—may help you to manage your moods by replacing pessimistic thoughts.

→ **Pray.** There's much evidence that prayer can make you feel better, even if you're not sure what to believe in.

Just choose

Sometimes no tricks are needed. You can simply *choose* optimism. Every morning as you head to work, you can *decide* to face the day with an optimistic attitude. Your elevated mood may not last, but each time a client is rude or your boss is unreasonable you'll have an opportunity to choose again. Throughout the day you'll have opportunities to let go of negativity and notice the positive. Some choices will be more challenging than others, but with repeated attempts at optimism your brain will change, and it will be increasingly easy to opt for the positive choice.

Learning how and why to be optimistic is something I've had to absorb more than once. Like everyone, I've had ups and downs. And I've discovered and rediscovered that managing my attitude must be part of my formula for working past the down times.

Choosing optimism is what I'm doing now, in this later phase of my professional life. I'm excited about the rapidly evolving new career options, and I'm electing to stay part of it all, rather than retire.

You also have the power to choose optimism in ways that can transform your career and enrich your life.

I wish you well.

BIBLIOGRAPHY

Allen, David. *Getting Things Done: The Art of Stress-Free Productivity*. New York: Penguin Books, 2001.

Baker, Dan, and Cameron Stauth. *What Happy People Know: How the New Science of Happiness Can Change Your Life for the Better*. Emmaus, PA: Rodale, 2003.

Begley, Sharon. *Train Your Mind, Change Your Brain: How a New Science Reveals Our Extraordinary Potential to Transform Ourselves*. New York: Ballantine Books, 2008.

Benson, Herbert, and William Proctor. *Beyond the Relaxation Response: How to Harness the Healing Power of Your Personal Beliefs*. New York: Times Books, 1984.

———. *The Breakout Principle: How to Activate the Natural Trigger that Maximizes Creativity, Productivity, and Personal Well-Being*. New York: Scribner, 2003.

Breuning, Loretta G. "What a Let-Down! When Your Happy Chemicals Dip, Your Brain Concocts Failure." *Psychology Today* (blog). Accessed October 10, 2014. https://www.psychologytoday.com/blog/your-neurochemical-self/201107/what-let-down.

Buckingham, Marcus, and Donald O. Clifton. *Now, Discover Your Strengths*. New York: Free Press, 2001.

Buettner, Dan. *The Blue Zones: Lessons for Living Longer from the People Who've Lived the Longest*. Washington, D.C.: National Geographic, 2008.

Buzan, Tony, and Barry Buzan. *The Mind Map Book: How to Use Radiant Thinking to Maximize Your Brain's Untapped Potential*. New York: Plume, 1993.

Carnegie, Dale. *How to Win Friends & Influence People*. New York: Pocket Books, 1998.

Carson, Richard David. *Taming Your Gremlin: A Surprisingly Simple Method for Getting out of Your Own Way*. New York: Quill, 2003.

Chaleff, Ira. *The Courageous Follower: Standing up to and for Our Leaders*. San Francisco: Berrett-Koehler Publishers, 1995.

Chopra, Deepak. *The Seven Spiritual Laws of Success: A Practical Guide to the Fulfillment of Your Dreams*. San Rafael, CA: Amber-Allen Publishing, 1994.

———. *The Spontaneous Fulfillment of Desire: Harnessing the Infinite Power of Coincidence*. New York: Harmony Books, 2003.

Chopra, Deepak, and Rudolph E. Tanzi. *Super Brain: Unleashing the Explosive Power of Your Mind to Maximize Health, Happiness, and Spiritual Well-Being*. New York: Harmony Books, 2012.

Collins, James C. *Good to Great: Why Some Companies Make the Leap—and Others Don't*. New York, NY: HarperBusiness, 2001.

Colvin, Geoffrey. *Talent Is Overrated: What Really Separates World-Class Performers from Everybody Else*. New York: Portfolio, 2008.

Covey, Stephen R. *The 8th Habit: From Effectiveness to Greatness*. Philadelphia: Running Press, 2006.

Coyle, Daniel. *The Little Book of Talent: 52 Tips for Improving Skills*. New York, NY: Bantam Books, 2012.

Cuddy, Amy. "Your body language shapes who you are." Accessed June 21, 2015. http://www.ted.com/talks/amy_cuddy_your_body_language_shapes_who _you_are.

Dalai Lama, and Howard C. Cutler. *The Art of Happiness: A Handbook for Living*. New York: Riverhead Books, 1998.

Davidson, Richard J., and Sharon Begley. *The Emotional Life of Your Brain: How Its Unique Patterns Affect the Way You Think, Feel, and Live—and How You Can Change Them*. New York: Hudson Street Press, 2012.

Dean, Jeremy. *Making Habits, Breaking Habits: How to Make Changes That Stick*. Richmond: Oneworld, 2013.

Drucker, Peter F. *The Age of Discontinuity: Guidelines to Our Changing Society*. New York: Harper & Row, 1969.

———. *Management: Tasks, Responsibilities, Practices*. New York: Harper & Row, 1974.

Duhigg, Charles. *The Power of Habit: Why We Do What We Do in Life and Business*. New York: Random House, 2012.

Dyer, Wayne W. *Excuses Begone!: How to Change Lifelong, Self-Defeating Thinking Habits*. Carlsbad, Calif.: Hay House, 2009.

Gallwey, W. Timothy, Edward S. Hanzelik, and John Horton. *The Inner Game of Stress: Outsmart Life's Challenges and Fulfill Your Potential*. New York: Random House, 2009.

Gerber, Michael E. *E-Myth Mastery: The Seven Essential Disciplines for Building a World Class Company*. New York: HarperCollins Publishers, 2005.

———. *The E-Myth Revisited: Why Most Small Businesses Don't Work and What to Do about It*. New York: CollinsBusiness, 1995.

Goleman, Daniel. *Emotional Intelligence*. New York: Bantam Books, 1995.

———. *Social Intelligence: The New Science of Human Relationships*. New York, NY: Bantam Books, 2007.

———. *The Brain and Emotional Intelligence: New Insights*. Northampton, MA: More Than Sound, 2011.

———. *Focus: The Hidden Driver of Excellence*. London: Bloomsbury, 2013.

Goulston, Mark. *Just Listen: Discover the Secret to Getting through to Absolutely Anyone*. New York: American Management Association, 2010.

Hannon, Kerry. *Great Jobs for Everyone 50+: Finding Work That Keeps You Happy and Healthy and Pays the Bills*. Hoboken, NJ: Wiley & Sons, 2012.

———. *What's Next?: Follow Your Passion and Find Your Dream Job*. San Francisco, Calif.: Chronicle Books, 2010.

———. *Love Your Job: The New Rules for Career Happiness*. Hoboken, NJ: Wiley & Sons, 2015.

Heath, Chip, and Dan Heath. *Made to Stick: Why Some Ideas Survive and Others Die*. New York: Random House, 2007.

———. *Switch: How to Change Things When Change Is Hard*. New York: Broadway Books, 2010.

Horstman, Judith. *The Scientific American Healthy Aging Brain: The Neuroscience of Making the Most of Your Mature Mind*. San Francisco: Jossey-Bass, 2012.

Iacoboni, Marco. *Mirroring People: The New Science of How We Connect with Others*. New York: Farrar, Straus and Giroux, 2008.

Jaworski, Joseph, and Betty S. Flowers. *Synchronicity: The Inner Path of Leadership*. San Francisco: Berrett-Koehler Publishers, 1996.

Jones, Beverly E. "No Girls Aloud: A Report on the 'report on the Status of Women at Ohio University' during the 1970s." 2005 Archives Lecture. Athens, Ohio. Lecture.

Koch, Richard. *The 80/20 Principle: The Secret to Success by Achieving More with Less*. New York: Currency, 1999.

Korda, Michael. *Horse People: Scenes from the Riding Life*. (Illustrations by the Author.) New York, NY: HarperCollins, 2003.

Kouzes, James M., and Barry Z. Posner. *The Leadership Challenge*. San Francisco, CA: Jossey-Bass, 2008.

LaFrance, Marianne. *Why Smile?: The Science Behind Facial Expressions*. New York: W.W. Norton, 2013.

Langer, Ellen J. *Counter Clockwise: Mindful Health and the Power of Possibility*. New York: Ballantine Books, 2009.

———. *Mindfulness*. Cambridge, MA: Lifelong Books/Da Capo Press, 2010.

Leonard, George. *Mastery: The Keys to Long-Term Success and Fulfillment*. New York, NY: Dutton, 1991.

Loehr, James E., and Tony Schwartz. *The Power of Full Engagement: Managing Energy, Not Time, Is the Key to High Performance and Personal Renewal*. New York: Free Press, 2005.

Maslow, Abraham H. *Motivation and Personality*. New York: Harper & Row, 1970.

McGonigal, Kelly. "How to make stress your friend." www.ted.com. June 2013.

Moore, Mark H. *Creating Public Value: Strategic Management in Government*. Cambridge, MA: Harvard University Press, 1995.

Norcross, John C., Kristin Loberg, and Jonathon Norcross. *Changeology: 5 Steps to Realizing Your Goals and Resolutions*. New York: Simon & Schuster, 2012.

Pantene. "Sorry, Not Sorry." Advertisement. Accessed June 18, 2014. https://www .youtube.com/watch?v=rzL-vdQ3ObA.

Pentland, Alex "Sandy". "The New Science of Building Great Teams." *Harvard Business Review*, April 2012. https://hbr.org/2012/04/the-new-science-of -building-great-teams/arl1.

Pink, Daniel H. *A Whole New Mind: Why Right-Brainers Will Rule the Future*. New York: Riverhead Books, 2006.

Pollan, Stephen M., and Mark Levine. *Second Acts: Creating the Life You Really Want, Building the Career You Truly Desire*. New York: HarperResource, 2003.

Price, Beverly Jones. *Report on the Status of Women at Ohio University*. Rep. no. 213296587. Athens, Ohio: Ohio U Libraries, 1972. Print.

Pritchard, Forrest, and Molly Peterson. *Growing Tomorrow: A Farm-To-Table Journey in Photos and Recipes: Behind the Scenes with 18 Extraordinary Sustainable Farmers Who Are Changing the Way We Eat*. New York: The Experiment, 2015.

Rahe, Richard, and Tores Theorell. "Workplace Stress." www.stress.org. The American Institute of Stress, June 2013. Web.

Rath, Tom, and Donald O. Clifton. *How Full Is Your Bucket?: Positive Strategies for Work and Life*. New York: Gallup Press, 2004.

Ryckman, Pamela. *Stiletto Network: Inside the Women's Power Circles That Are Changing the Face of Business*. New York: AMACOM, 2013.

Sandberg, Sheryl, and Nell Scovell. *Lean In: Women, Work, and the Will to Lead*. New York: Knopf, 2013.

Seligman, Martin E.P. *What You Can Change and What You Can't*. New York: Vintage Books, 1993.

———. *Authentic Happiness: Using the New Positive Psychology to Realize Your Potential for Lasting Fulfillment*. New York: Free Press, 2002.

———. *Learned Optimism: How to Change Your Mind and Your Life*. New York: Vintage Books, 2006.

Silverman, Craig. *Regret the Error: How Media Mistakes Pollute the Press and Imperil Free Speech*. New York: Union Square Press, 2007.

Strozzi-Heckler, Richard. *Holding the Center: Sanctuary in a Time of Confusion*. Berkeley, Calif.: Frog, 1997.

Sweeney, Camille, and Josh Gosfield. *The Art of Doing: How Superachievers Do What They Do and How They Do It so Well*. New York: Penguin Group, 2013.

Tracy, Brian. *Eat That Frog*. Offenbach: GABAL, 2002.

"Twenty-five Best-Mannered People of 2014." The National League of Junior Cotillions. Accessed January 2, 2015. http://www.nljc.com/tenbest mannered.html.

Watkins, Michael. *The First 90 Days: Critical Success Strategies for New Leaders at All Levels*. Boston, MA: Harvard Business School Press, 2003.

Wheeler, Claire Michaels. *10 Simple Solutions to Stress: How to Tame Tension & Start Enjoying Your Life*. Oakland, Calif.: New Harbinger Publications, 2007.

Whyte, William Hollingsworth. *The Organization Man*. New York: Simon and Schuster, 1956.

Winston, Stephanie. *Organized for Success: Top Executives and CEOs Reveal the Organizing Principles That Helped Them Reach the Top*. New York, NY: Crown Business, 2004.

Zander, Rosamund Stone, and Benjamin Zander. *The Art of Possibility*. New York: Penguin Books, 2002.

INDEX

DRESSING BEST
TOP to Bottom } CREAT
CONFIDENT

NETWORK = MASTERMENT
= Associate
= FREINS

ABOUT THE AUTHOR

Beverly Jones is a master of reinvention. She led university programs for women before trailblazing her career as a Washington lawyer and Fortune 500 energy executive. Throughout her varied work life she has mentored other professionals and leaders to grow and thrive.

Since 2002, Jones has been a respected executive coach and leadership consultant, helping professionals of all ages to advance their careers, shift directions, and become more productive. Based in the nation's capital, she works with clients spread across the country, including accomplished leaders in Congress, at major federal agencies, NGOs, universities, large corporations, and small businesses.

Jones is a popular speaker and facilitator, and creates workshops and retreats around the needs of her clients. She is a visiting executive with Ohio University's Voinovich School of Leadership and Public Affairs. Her podcasts are distributed through WOUB Digital, and her blog posts and e-zine archive are found on her Website: *www.clearwaysconsulting.com*. Jones is active on Twitter: @beverlyejones.